RECENT STUDIES IN
PHILOSOPHY AND THEOLOGY

INTERNATIONAL LIBRARY OF
PHILOSOPHY AND THEOLOGY

PHILOSOPHICAL AND HISTORICAL STUDIES SERIES

Rousas J. Rushdoony, *Editor*

RECENT STUDIES
IN
PHILOSOPHY
and
THEOLOGY

By
DAVID HUGH FREEMAN

BAKER BOOK HOUSE—GRAND RAPIDS 6, MICHIGAN
1962

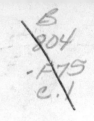
© Copyright 1962
By the Presbyterian and Reformed Publishing Co.
Philadelphia, Penna.

Library of Congress Catalog Card Number 62-21164

Printed in the United States of America

To the memory of my mother, Grace Kern Freeman, whose devotion, encouragement, understanding, and patience helped to make this book possible.

Foreword

Dr. Freeman's book deals with a problem which is both of eternal significance and of the greatest actuality. It is as grave as it is inescapable. Dr. Freeman discusses the solutions of this problem proposed by Maritain, Gilson, Dooyeweerd, Tillich and the analytical and linguistic philosophers of today. His arguments are deep and compelling, mostly so with respect to the present nominalists, least, I think, with respect to Tillich. His book is a necessary and wholesome antidote against nihilistic currents of thought and I hope it will be carefully studied and considered by the adherents of this school.

Richard Kroner

Philadelphia, June 1962

ACKNOWLEDGEMENTS

The author wishes to express his gratitude to Professor Francis Clarke of the University of Pennsylvania for his friendly advice and encouragement; to Professor Richard Kroner, for his generous criticisms; to his colleagues, Wm. Oliver Martin and William Young, for many hours of discussion which helped to shape parts of the book; and to John Murphy for his painstaking reading of the proofs and his constructive criticism.

He is especially indebted to Rousas J. Rushdoony for including this work in the *Philosophical and Historical Studies* series in the International Library of Philosophy and Theology.

David Hugh Freeman

September, 1962
Kingston, R. I.

Contents

Introduction

During the past fifty years various attempts have been made to establish the relationship between philosophy and Christian theology. To determine this relationship, it is necessary to define each. However, there is no universal agreement as to the meaning of these terms. The present work is a critical examination of several contemporary points of view of this relationship.

The encounter of philosophy with Christian theology discloses at least three basic attitudes toward the relationship of philosophy to theology. The first is negative to any philosophical tradition developed outside of the Christian revelation. Athens and Jerusalem are thought to have nothing in common. Philosophy is no concern to the Christian believer. Since the Bible contains the detailed answers to philosophical and scientific problems, the Christian faith is not in need of reason; it is itself a substitute for philosophy.

The second attitude regards philosophy as an autonomous discipline completely independent of theology. Here theological speculation presupposes faith and is primarily concerned with grace, whereas philosophical activity depends solely on reason, and is primarily concerned with nature. The hostility of the

first attitude is absent in the second; philosophy and theology
are here considered capable of offering each other assistance.

The third attitude seeks to unite "faith" and "reason" into
a single whole. For Augustine knowledge is unattainable except
by faith,[1] since faith precedes understanding. One does not seek
to understand, in order to believe, but one must believe in order
to understand.[2] The priority of faith over reason and the necessity of faith for knowledge is an essential feature of Augustine's
writings and the tradition that he has inspired.

The Augustinian is firm in adhering to the words of Augustine when he writes: "We believe in order to know; for if we
wanted to know first and then to believe, we should not be able
either to know or to believe."[3] Philosophical understanding is
not to be condemned by faith but the latter is to so "purify thee
—that understanding may fill thee."[4]

For I not only judge it most healthful to believe before reason,
when you are not qualified to receive reason, and by the very act of
faith thoroughly to cultivate the mind to receive the seeds of truth,
but altogether a thing of such sort so that without it (faith) health
cannot return to sick souls.[5]

Philosophy and theology may be related to each other in such
a manner that both philosophy and theology are viewed as
scientific disciplines which are capable of yielding knowledge of
actual states of affairs. But a theologian may also refuse to accept the truth claims of philosophy, and a philosopher may
refuse to recognize the statements of a theologian. And it is
also possible that someone else may refuse to recognize either
philosophy or theology as cognitive disciplines. In other words,
one may accept or reject philosophy and theology as cognitive
and meaningful, or one may accept theology and reject philosophy, or accept philosophy and reject theology. However,
even when both philosophy and theology are accepted, there is

[1] Cf. Augustine, *Expositions on the Book of Psalms*, Schaff ed. Vol. viii, p. 29.
[2] *Tractate* xxix, Schaff, Vol. vii, 1.
[3] *Tractate* xxvii, chap. vi, 9.
[4] *Tractate* xxxvii, 7.
[5] *De Utilitate Credendi*, Schaff, Vol. III, p. 362.

still no general agreement among philosophers and theologians as to what is the proper object of their investigation.

The philosopher may view philosophy as a means by which metaphysical knowledge is attainable, or he may restrict it to an analysis of certain forms of human experience. And the theologian may view theology as a means by which metaphysical knowledge of an ultimate being is attained, or he may restrict it to an analysis of religious experience.

The present work does not seek to give an exhaustive definition of either philosophy or theology, and yet, it attempts to partially define philosophy and theology, and their relationship to each other. It contains a partial description of what philosophers and theologians have done in the past and continue to do when they claim to be at work.

Whether or not what philosophers and theologians try to do is capable of being done needs to be considered. Some people reject both philosophy and theology; others reject either philosophy or theology. Among the many reasons for rejecting philosophy, the main objection is, perhaps, that it has nothing to offer. If knowledge is obtainable at all, then it must be obtained by one of the sciences. Philosophy is simply a vestige of bygone ages, and the scientific method is the only method capable of yielding knowledge.

Critics of this objection to philosophy might well point out that to deny the legitimacy of philosophy on the ground that the scientific method is the only method by which anything can be known, is to make certain assumptions which traditionally have been called philosophical. Indeed, to hold that the scientific method of observation and experiment is the only method capable of yielding knowledge is a philosophical assumption rather than a datum of science.

The scientific method would be the only method, if it were the case that everything that is, is observable, at least in principle. If the world is all that there is, if everything that is, is matter, then, of course, the concepts of the natural sciences are to date the best that can be offered. Whether the world is all that there is, and whether the ultimate nature of the world is material, ideal or something else, is, however, precisely the kind of thing about which philosophers and theologians talk.

The statement: "The scientific method of observation and experiment is the only method of yielding knowledge about matters of fact" is itself not discovered by the scientific method of observation and experiment. If by "matters of fact" what is meant is "what is observable," the proposition simply states that the "method of observation is the only way of observing what is observable." And this is obviously the case. To observe one must observe.

The statement under consideration is equally innocuous, if it is taken as an expression of interest, as a way of saying that what I am interested in, is what science can do by means of the method of science. If what is meant, however, is that what is, is what is observable, then such an assumption is a judgment about the nature of the universe, and it is hard to see how a metaphysical position can be used to deny that philosophy is possible.

It is well to note that much confusion arises from simply talking about what philosophy does. Philosophy has never done anything, but then neither has physics. For neither philosophy nor physics are of such a nature that they can do things, in the same way that football players can tackle and cats can grin.

Philosophy does not have knowledge any more than physics does. To speak of what philosophy does or knows is to speak loosely. A person who calls himself a philosopher or a physicist may know something. But neither philosophy, nor physics knows or does anything.

What is it that a philosopher might know that is peculiar to him as a philosopher? Knowledge consists of propositions, that is, of statements that are true or false. If the philosopher knows certain propositions which he has systematized and arranged, and if such propositions are different from the propositions of any of the separate sciences, the sum total of such propositions could then be said to constitute a body of knowledge, and such a body of knowledge could then be called philosophy. But are there really any propositions which are different from the propositions of any of the special sciences? There are such statements, namely, the statements made *about* a particular science. Such statements may be about the method and the importance of a science, or they may be about its relationship to another science or to all the other sciences.

Some philosophers may restrict themselves to making statements about the sciences, about their language, method, and inter-relationship. Such a restriction may simply be a matter of personal interest. It may, however, stem from the conviction that there is nothing more to know.

Other philosophers are interested in doing more than making statements about the interrelationship between the sciences. They ask questions about God, man, and the world that are not asked or answered by any of the sciences. It may be that all or some of the statements that some philosophers make are false, obscure, or confused, but it is undeniable that they make them.

The term "knowledge" is ambiguous. It is used to refer to the sum total of all the propositions which we hold to be true and which really are true. It is also used to refer to all the propositions which we hold to be true and which may or may not be true. And when certain propositions are systematized and arranged in an orderly fashion, according to their subject matter, we then use the term "knowledge" to refer to one or more of these special groupings, and speak of the sciences.

It is not necessary to insist that all the propositions that constitute philosophy are true. No such claim could be made for any body of knowledge, including the natural sciences. It is absurd to maintain that all philosophical statements are true, for many contradict each other. To admit that there are philosophical propositions, and to admit that they contradict, is to admit that some philosophical statements are true. Two contradictory statements cannot both be false. Which statement is true, and which statement is false, is another matter.

Anyone who rejects philosophy as a separate field of knowledge must of necessity hold that there are no genuine philosophical propositions. Everyone is not willing to make so sweeping an assertion.

The situation is quite different with respect to theology. Although no one doubts that there have been people who called themselves theologians, is there a body of true propositions which can properly be termed theological?

The question, "Is theology possible?," is closely connected to the question, "Is revelation possible?" For while the term theology may refer to man's speculations about God, to the history of religion, and to comparative religion, yet, within the Biblical tradition, "theology" designates a separate science, with its own field of investigation. Christian theologians seek to investigate and systematize the revelation of God. Christian theologians presuppose that God has taken the initiative in making himself known, so that they can know what God requires of man by studying his revealed word.

The question as to whether there is revelation is a meaningful question, at least in the sense that it is readily understood, even by most of those that answer it negatively. Of course, those who hold that God exists are apt to be more interested in the question than those who do not. Interest, however, is a personal matter; it has nothing to do with the importance of a question. The question of revelation may be of tremendous importance, even though genuine interest in it may frequently be hard to find.

There are many reasons why people lose interest. If the answer is already known, there is little point in further inquiry. One reason why people no longer concern themselves with the problem of revelation is that they live under the illusion that they have already solved it. It is somehow thought that a negative answer is the only possible answer.

A truly critical attitude calls for a careful investigation before giving an answer. It is quite possible to reach a negative answer as to whether or not there is revelation, even after the question has received careful consideration. It is, however, dogmatic either to ignore the question or to dismiss it in an arbitrary manner.

Those who have never considered the question of revelation might well reflect on the historical fact that for hundreds of years, learned men held to the common conviction that men could and did have a knowledge of God which was the result of the initiative of God. What facts have since been discovered that demonstrate that such initiative was never taken?

It would be fallacious to seek to prove the fact of revelation by means of an examination of Western civilization. The task of establishing causal relations in history is extremely difficult. The historical situation, past and present, is relevant to the problem but not definitive.

Interest in the question of revelation may be reawakened, however, by considering certain historical developments within the Western world. The reader is undoubtedly familiar with the story. For centuries revelation and reason were both accepted as means by which God was known with, at times, a greater emphasis placed upon the one rather than the other. The assumption was commonly held, however, that, when properly interpreted, revealed truth and truths of reason were never in conflict. This state of harmony did not last forever. With the dawn of modern times, the certainty that there could be no conflict between the truth of revelation and of reason vanished. The harmony was broken. Some chose the side of reason, others of revelation. Some held to revelation, but limited its voice, ascribing to reason alone the task of constructing a certain picture of the world.

Man now ascribed to his own personality the free sovereign creative power that he previously had ascribed to God. With mathematics as his model, he proceeded to create his own world, a world which later seemed to have little room for his new found freedom, since his own personality was ever threatened by the alleged scientific view of the world that he, himself, was in the process of creating.

The seventeenth century in general did not deny the fact of

revelation. It simply made it unimportant. Reason was all that was really needed. The eighteenth century retained its trust in reason, but now revelation came under direct attack. God and morality were to be retained to the extent that they were compatible with reason. However, toward the end of the 18th Century, Kant put an end to man's reliance on reason. What began with a rejection of the importance of revelation, in the name of reason, ended in a rejection of *both* reason and revelation.

The rejection of a revealed God ended in the rejection of the God of reason. Whether this process was accidental or causal may be debatable. But it is clear that something has happened in what has been called our post-modern, post-Christian era. The story is not complete. There is a correlation between whatever a man thinks of God and what he thinks of himself. When man believed that God was the creator, he regarded himself as a creature.

As long as man believed in a revealed God, he could turn to what was revealed about God and learn about himself. He could learn what he should do to glorify God, and, since God was believed to be holy and just, his own conduct was prescribed by the very nature of God. His conduct was determined for him by God's holy law, found for both Christians and Jews in the decalogue.

At first, even when a revealed God was rejected, it was still thought that man had a nature, and that certain rights were guaranteed to him by the author of his nature. The God of reason remained, and standards of conduct could still be had by understanding what conduct would complete or perfect man's nature.

The situation remained unchanged, from a practical point of view, even after Feuerbach, for example, rejected the existence of God. For he still held that man had a nature and that there are unchanging moral standards.

It was not until the end of the nineteenth century that human nature and moral standards were discarded together with the notion of a revealed God. Man now derived his nature from the group to which he belonged. He became a part of the herd, or one of the leaders. His nature and his conduct now depended upon the group to which he belongs, upon his purposes, upon the "values" that he adopts. There is now no longer any agreement as to what man is, as to what he should do, nor as to how he should behave. Some would let him do whatever most people want to do. Others would subordinate his interests to those of the state or a party. Some simply wait gloomily for the giant mushroom cloud that may put an end to further debate within the Western world.

Under what conditions would it be possible for theology to have a special field of investigation? Theology could be a science if the proposition "God has revealed himself" is true.

There are several conditions that would render the above proposition false. It would be false if the concept of God referred to by the word "God" failed to designate anything outside of the world of concepts. If God has no objective existence, the statement "God reveals" cannot truly mean what it means for orthodox believers. If there is no being capable of revealing, then the statement that such a being reveals is simply false. It is then false for the same reason that the statement "Leprechauns drink milk," is false, i.e., there are no Leprechauns.

There is a second reason why the proposition "God has revealed himself" could be false. It might be held that although God exists, there is something about the nature of God that either makes it impossible for God to reveal himself, or more simply, that although he could, if he wanted to, there is, however, no evidence that he is at all interested in so doing. In short, the proposition is false simply because God has not revealed himself, at least not in the special way that orthodox Christians, for example, talk about.

Of course, some may even be willing to admit that, given the existence of God, there is a certain sense in which it can be said that God reveals. If you simply mean that God's existence is somehow evident within my mind, or from the nature of the external world, then in this general sense, God may be said to reveal, but if you mean more than that, the proposition is false.

The proposition "God reveals himself" is thus equivalent in meaning to the proposition "man is aware of God."

It is evident that the words "reveal" and "revelation" can refer to different concepts. What the orthodox religious believer means when he says "God reveals himself" is that it is God who is active. The word "reveal" here refers to something that God does, and not simply to a human awareness of God. Before answering the question as to whether the proposition "God has revealed himself" is a true proposition, it is first necessary to clarify what is comprehended in the concept of "revealing." What does the orthodox believer mean?

But first, what is ordinarily understood by an act of revealing under circumstances other than religious ones? There are certain necessary conditions without which an act of revealing does not take place. One prerequisite for such an act is *ignorance*. In order for X to reveal something to Y, Y must first be ignorant of what X reveals. If Y already knows what X says, then X simply tells Y what Y already knows and X then does not reveal anything to Y. Ignorance on the part of Y is thus a necessary, although not a sufficient condition for an act of revealing to take place. Before there can be an act of revealing, there must also be some person or persons that are related in some way to Y. Unless there is an X with whom Y is in contact, there can be no act of revealing. And in the third place, an act of revealing can take place, if and only if, X reveals *something* to Y, something that Y previously did not know. An act of revealing removes some initial ignorance. X reveals S (something) to Y. But this still does not exhaust what is ordinarily meant by the word "reveal." On occasion Y may learn something from X by accident. And the word "reveal" is sometimes used in this somewhat restricted sense: that X discloses something to Y unintentionally. There is a stronger usage, however, and it is this stronger sense that is of importance to our problem. In a somewhat stronger sense, X is said to reveal something to Y when X does so intentionally, that is, when X has a purpose (P). It is, moreover, not to be overlooked that when X reveals something to Y for a purpose (P), he does so at a particular time and place (T) by certain means (M). In this strong sense then, an act of revealing takes place solely between persons, for persons alone are capable of having conscious purposes, at least on a high level of complexity.

An act of revealing thus takes place when X reveals S to Y for purpose (P) by means of M at a time and place (T). What is thus transmited to Y may then be referred to as the revelation of X to Y.

It is this strong usage of the word "reveal" that is in question when orthodox Christians, for example, utter the statement "God has revealed himself."

And for this proposition to be true, one must be able to assign an intelligible meaning to X, S, Y, P, M, T. If one of the conditions is not met, the proposition "God has revealed himself" cannot be a true proposition in the strong sense of "revealed."

Let us continue our analysis in more detail. God can be truly said to have revealed himself if, and only if, there is a God, our previous X. But the mere fact that God exists does not constitute an act of revealing. It is presumed by theologians that God was before the existence of the world, before there was any person or being to whom he could reveal himself. God can only be said to reveal himself to some one (Y). And if God has revealed himself to Y, in this case to some human being then God has revealed something (S) to Y, something which Y did not know before. And since accidental behavior is hardly to be ascribed to what men understand by "God," it is to be assumed that whatever God does is purposeful (P). It is equally obvious that if God is to reveal himself to men (Y), he must do so at a certain time and place (T) by means (M) that are intelligible to Y. If all such conditions have in fact been met, then it can be truly said that "God has revealed himself." The expression "the special revelation of God" can then be used to refer to all such acts of revealing that satisfy the conditions X, S, Y, P, M, and T. Stated in a more formal way, one can say that there is divine revelation if, and only if, all the conditions X, S, Y, P, M, and T are satisfied where X refers to God, S refers to what is made known, Y to those persons to whom S is made known, P, for the purpose X has in making S known to Y, and M stands for the means used by X to make S known to Y, and T stands for the time and place where X made S known to Y by means of M for purpose P.

The question as to whether God has in fact revealed himself is distinct from the question as to whether it is possible that God could have revealed himself. The possibility of revelation might be granted, while the actuality of revelation might be denied. It is also to be remembered that even if it is granted that God could and did reveal himself, this still would not decide the question as to where and when such actual revelation occurred.

Unless such revelation has occurred, it is impossible to have a theology in the sense of the systematic study of revelation.

The present work considers three contemporary views of the relation between philosophy and theology, the neo-Thomism of Etienne Gilson and Jacques Maritain, the neo-Augustinianism of Herman Dooyeweerd, and the views of Paul Tillich. It will become apparent that Dooyeweerd and the neo-Thomists share the common belief that God has revealed himself, but they differ as to what philosophy is and how it is to be related to theology. Tillich, on the other hand, differs from both the neo-Thomists and Dooyeweerd on the nature of philosophy and of theology.

The first three chapters of this volume treat the relationship between philosophy and theology in the neo-Thomism of Gilson and Maritain, the neo-Augustinianism of Herman Dooyeweerd, and the neo-Existentialism of Paul Tillich. The fourth chapter is devoted to a critical comparison of the material in chapters one to three in terms of the basic presuppositions of the positions considered.

The fifth and final chapter critically examines several objections that could be raised against the possibility of theology.

RECENT STUDIES IN
PHILOSOPHY AND THEOLOGY

I. The Neo-Thomism of Gilson and Maritain

Neo-Thomism's General Indebtedness to Aquinas

Neo-Thomism signifies a common conviction with respect to being, knowing, God, the world, and man; however, there is a great diversity of opinion within this framework.

The more conservative Thomists are inclined to find a system of truth available within the writings of St. Thomas, and consider it their task to exposit and explain his doctrine. To this group belong Th. Pegues, A. D. Sertillanges, A. Doodkorte, and J. de Tonquedéc.

The more progressive Thomists consider Thomas' philosophy to be the most adequate expression of human knowledge in the field of philosophy. But they do not regard it as a closed system; its value consists in its principles which permit an independent solution to problems of which Thomas himself may have been unaware. To this group belong A. Gemelli, R. Garrigou-Lagrange, M. D. Roland-Gosselin, P. Rousselot, R. Jolivet, A. Forest, J. Maritain, V. Cathrein, T. Pesch, Maria Laach, J. Mausbach, J. Geyser, J. Beysens, J. Hoogveld, I. Van den Berg, J. Maher, R. Clarke, L. Walker, H. Robbers, and Wm. Oliver Martin.

1

A third group of Thomists have primarily concerned them-
selves with historical studies; e.g., M. Grabmann, Cl. Baeumker,
B. Geyer, F. Pelster, E. Gilson, G. Théry, M. D. Chenu, M.
DeWolf, F. Van Steenbergen, J. de Ghellinek, and O. Lottin.[1]

We do not intend to discuss the various contributions and
differences between the aforementioned philosophers. Instead
we shall limit ourselves to the writings of Gilson, Maritain,
and St. Thomas.

The Neo-Thomist is indebted to St. Thomas for his conception of the relation between faith and reason, his view of God,
and the way in which God is knowable.

Thomas taught that the truth of the Christian faith exceeds
man's rational ability but human reason cannot be opposed to
it, since true faith and true knowledge can only be in agreement. God has endowed man with natural knowledge and what
is known by faith is divinely revealed, so that rational arguments
against the faith, are either probable or sophistical and can
therefore be answered.[2] And although some truths exceed
human reason, e.g., that God is triune, the light of natural
reason is able to demonstrate that God exists and that he is one.[3]

The divine substance is not comprehensible to the human
intellect, for the knowledge of the latter originates in the senses,
and is restricted to what can be gathered from sensible things.
Only the divine intellect fully understands what it is. Although
the truth concerning the divine being is twofold, one to
which reason can reach, the other surpassing reason, it is not
superfluous for God to reveal what is also knowable to reason,
since otherwise few would possess knowledge of God, owing to
their lack of interest, lack of time, and limited ability.[4]

The philosopher is concerned with the nature of things in
themselves, and the theologian with things in their relation

---

[1] Cf. F. Sassen, *Wysbegerte von onze Tijd* (Antwerpen: N. V. Standaard-
Boekhandel, 1944), pp. 251, 278.

[2] St. Thomas Aquinas, *Summa Contra Gentiles*, Bk. I, trans. Anton C. Pegis
(New York: Image Books, 1944), pp. 74-75.

[3] *Ibid.*, p. 63.

[4] *Ibid.*, pp. 66, 69.

to God, although theology may use philosophical elements for theological ends.

"The revealed" for Thomas is not accessible to reason, and since the knowledge of philosophy does not exceed the limits of reason, it cannot belong to "the revealed," but it may belong to the *revelabilia* (the revealable); that is, natural knowledge may be included in revelation since man needs to know it for salvation.[5]

The wise man has the task of ordering things rightly, and the absolutely wise man is concerned with the end of the universe, which is at the same time its origin. The ultimate end of the wise man is truth, and first of all philosophy is the science of truth. And truth is accessible to faith and to reason.[6] For man requires knowledge of the true God if he is to know the truth, and faith thus confers perfection and consummation on rational knowledge. To know God truly is to believe that he is above what man can think about him. The influence of faith on reason permits more fruitful rational activity. Reason advances, therefore, under the beneficient action of faith, so that the relation between faith and reason is intimate, although they are not to be confused.

Because philosophy argues from the essence of things, from their proper causes, it differs from theology in its principles of demonstration. For the theologian argues from God, the first cause of all things, and affirms a truth on the principle of authority, or because the glory or infinite power of God demands it. Thus the demonstration of the philosopher is based on reason, and follows a different order, proceeding from a consideration of the creature to God, whereas in the doctrine of faith the consideration of God precedes the consideration of the creature.[7]

Gilson and Maritain follow Thomas in maintaining that the degrees of rational knowledge depend upon reason alone, while at the same time recognizing a higher light which is to be

---

[5] E. Gilson, *The Christian Philosophy of St. Thomas Aquinas* (New York: Random House, 1956), pp. 11-15.

[6] Aquinas, *Summa Contra Gentiles,* pp. 59-63.

[7] Gilson, *op. cit.,* p. viii.

joined to reason.[8] For faith exercises an external and negative control preventing the philosopher from falling into errors against revealed doctrine, and in the order of its exercise, philosophy is given a positively Christian character by Christian revelation and the enlightenment present in the philosopher due to grace.[9]

Wisdom is thus threefold, the infused wisdom of grace, which attains God in love and union, and knows God by the illumination of the divine; theological wisdom, the communication of the knowledge of God by revelation, the wisdom of faith, and of faith making use of reason; and metaphysical wisdom, with its own special light, i.e., the intelligibility of being in its pure state.[10]

Revelation is, however, not a substitute for science and metaphysics. That God has spoken does not imply that we are in need of nothing else. The neo-Thomist does not seek to reach truth by proceedings from revelation to reason;[11] he would replace the Augustinian principle, "unless you believe, you shall not understand," by an effort to harmonize reason and revelation. And, although his religious faith rests upon the unshakable certitude that God has spoken, metaphysical knowledge rests solely upon rational and necessary demonstrations,[12] so that philosophy is not a department of theology,[13] and although philosophy may be related to the latter, is may not be reduced to it. For philosophical truth is not based on revelation but on reason. And an agreement between philosophy and theology cannot be reached by forgetting the essential difference between the two.[14]

In each instance of philosophical thinking, philosophy is con-

[8] Jacques Maritain, *The Degrees of Knowledge* (New York: Scribners, 1938), p. xiii.

[9] Jacques Maritain, *Science and Wisdom* (New York: Scribners, 1940), p. viii.

[10] *Ibid.*, pp. 22-23.

[11] E. Gilson, *Reason and Revelation in the Middle Ages* (New York: Scribner's Sons, 1938), p. 17.

[12] *Ibid.*, pp. 77 ff.

[13] E. Gilson, *The Unity of Philosophical Experience* (New York: Scribners, 1937), pp. 49 ff.

[14] *Ibid.*, p. 62.

cerned with finding the first cause of all that is.[15] Man is by nature a metaphysical animal, that is to say, he is rational by nature; he has a natural propensity to transcend the limits of experience. The knowledge acquired by metaphysics is acquired by a naturally transcendent reason,[16] for metaphysics seeks to transcend all particular knowledge,[17] since its first principle is being. Consequently, the failures of metaphysics are due to the misuse or misunderstanding of its first principle.[18]

Neo-Thomism is characterized by a return to metaphysics, a return to the notion of being.[19] And the neo-Thomist is not bothered by the positivist criticism of metaphysics. He admits that the assertions made by the scientist are not concerned with the substance of things, with the nature or essence of what is, but he holds that it is erroneous to assume that what is of no meaning to the scientist has no meaning at all.[20] For knowledge is dependent upon what is, and what is, is independent of my knowledge,[21] and science is not identical with human wisdom.[22] A scientific definition fails to tell us what a thing is. It simply enables us to agree on its characterizations and measurements and provides a knowledge of the manner in which the signs referring to its impact on experience can be grouped in a coherent language.[23]

Neo-Thomism would place us in a world of the eternal and the absolute by investigating a world of realities entirely separate from matter. Its object is the cause of all causes, the principle of everything that is. In short, metaphysics enables us to know God.[24]

Metaphysics is the supreme science of the natural order. It

[15] *Ibid.*, p .306.
[16] *Ibid.*, p. 308.
[17] *Ibid.*, p. 310.
[18] *Ibid.*, p. 316.
[19] Gilson, *The Christian Philosophy of St. Thomas Aquinas*, p. 357.
[20] Jacques Maritain, *The Range of Reason* (New York: Scribner's Sons, 1952), pp. 5 ff.
[21] *Ibid.*, p. 12.
[22] Maritain, *Science and Wisdom*, p. 31.
[23] Maritain, *The Range of Reason*, p. 6.
[24] Maritain, *The Degrees of Knowledge*, pp. 9 ff.

transcends experience and reaches a super-experimental knowledge which is absolutely certain, thereby supplying the framework of the sciences without doing violence to their internal development.[25]

Metaphysical knowledge is possible because the mind is able to deal with what is beyond sensible nature, with being as being. Its objects cannot only be conceived without matter but they can exist without it. Knowledge of sensory nature removes only contingent and strictly individual particulars. Such objects do not exist apart from matter, nor can they be conceived apart from it.[26] Metaphysics rises above visible things and recognizes by reasoning the existence of God, as the first cause and the author of nature. His existence, perfections, unity, simplicity, and the real and absolute distinction between him and the world may be known by reasons drawn from created things so that God may be known by knowing perfections analogically common to the uncreated and the created.[27]

The Proofs of the Existence of God

The traditional arguments for the existence of God as formulated by Aquinas are of central significance to our problem. The problem of the existence of God, as viewed by the Thomist, presupposes an understanding of the term "existence." Thomas distinguishes two aspects of the real, an *ens,* a being, and *esse,* the very act of being. The term "substance" refers to the *entia* or beings which appear in sense experience and which form a complete whole with an analyzable structure constituting an ontological unit capable of definition. A substance susceptible of definition is called "essence," so that essence is what the definition says the substance is. To the degree that an essence is expressed in a definition, it is called a *quiddity.* Thus a concrete ontological unit taken in itself is substance; taken as susceptible of definition it is essence; and taken as signified by the definition, it is quiddity.[28] Substance is therefore an essence or

[25] *Ibid.,* pp. 83 ff.
[26] *Ibid.,* pp. 45 ff.
[27] *Ibid.,* pp. 306 ff.
[28] Gilson, *The Christian Philosophy of St. Thomas Aquinas,* p. 30.

quiddity which exists by itself in virtue of its own act of being. The problem of being and of beings known as substances is concerned with actual existence. For substances are units of existence. But substance does not exist by itself independently of a cause of its existence, but in the sense that what is in it belongs to it by virtue of an act of existing.

Sensible things are the only substances of which we have direct experience. And these substances can be distributed into classes which are the objects of concepts which in turn can be expressed by definition. Thus the datum of our sensible experience can be conceptualized. And it is the form of the substance which makes conceptual knowledge of the real possible. Every substance implies a form which enables it to be classified in a species, but the latter do not exist as such. Individuals are the only substances known. The members of the same species are therefore distinguished from each other, not by their form, but by another element of the real, matter.[29] Matter is not the cause of the existence of a substance; it is only a potency determinable by the form. For it is that by which the substance is that which is. As a unity of form and matter, each substance is an *ens,* a something which is. A problem concerning substance is therefore a problem of being. An explanation of a being as a substance explains why this being is what it is. But after explaining why a being is what it is, a further explanation is needed; an explanation which explains what makes it exist. Concrete substances, the objects of sensible experience, contain two metaphysical levels, that of matter and form, constituting the substantiality of substance, and that of substance with its act of existing, which constitutes the substance as "being" because it is thereby an existing thing. The problem of the relation of the essence to its act-of-being (*esse*) arises for all beings whose essence is not to exist. Consequently, the existence of things known empirically is in need of explanation. A being whose essence is not its act of being does not itself have the wherewithal to exist. Thus the distinction between essence and the act-of-

---

[29] *Ibid.,* pp. 31, 32.

existing poses the problem of the cause of finite existence, the problem of the existence of God.[30]

It is, however, impossible and superfluous to demonstrate the existence of God if his existence is self-evident. That the latter is the case has been affirmed by those who hold that the proposition "God exists" is known as soon as we know its terms, since the name of God means something than which a greater cannot be conceived, and this notion is immediately formed in the intellect, and cannot exist solely there, since to exist in the intellect and in reality is greater than to exist in the intellect alone. The very definition of the name of God thus implies his existence.[31] If God himself could be thought not to be, then something greater than God could be thought.

The contrary to the proposition "God exists" cannot be entertained by the mind. God is that through which intelligible knowledge is possible. And if anything is true, truth must exist, and God is truth itself. The desire of man naturally tends toward God. His being is his essence, so that in the proposition "God exists," the predicate is identical with or included in the subject.[32]

But all arguments that God's existence is self-evident mistake for God what is only an effect caused by God. What is innate is not the knowledge that God exists but the reason by which we can return to God via his effects. Existence needs to be demonstrated, not deduced.[33]

The mind clings by habit to what it has been taught as something natural and self-evident. But it is necessary to distinguish what is absolutely self-evident, and what is self-evident to us. The existence of God is self-evident in itself since what God is is his own being, but since we cannot conceive what God is, that he exists remains unknown to us. The being we know is

[30] *Ibid.*, p. 36.

[31] *Summa Contra Gentiles*, Bk. 1, Chap., 10.

[32] St. Thomas Aquinas, *Summa Theologica.* trans. by the Fathers of the English Dominican Province (London: Burns, Oates and Washbourne, Ltd., 1922), I, 2, 1, obj. 3; and *Summa Contra Gentiles*, I, 10.

[33] Gilson, *The Christian Philosophy of St. Thomas*, pp. 54-55.

not that of God, since every object of experience needs God as its cause. The existence of God can be demonstrated with certainty but it is not the result of an intuition. Man can only return to God by starting with the knowledge of his effects. Because we are unable to see his essence, we do not arrive at the knowledge of his being through God himself. Our knowledge is caused through his influence, through reason—by way of the likenesses of God found in his effects. It is simply false that the meaning of God's name implies the knowledge of his existence. There is no agreement that God is that than which a greater cannot be conceived, and even if this were universally understood by the name of God, it does not follow that in reality such exists, and not simply in the intellect. The existence of God is not evident *a priori*.[34]

The possibility of demonstrating the existence of God is further called into question by those who believe that faith and revelation are the sole avenue to God. Thomas admits that God transcends sensible things but still believes that his existence can be demonstrated by examining his effects, so that we can have knowledge of what transcends the sensory.[35]

The existence of God is thus not an article of faith but a preamble to faith; as grace presupposes nature, so faith presupposes reason.[36]

Thomas' first and most obvious way to God is based upon the argument from motion. It is evident to our senses that some things are in motion. And what is moved is moved by another. Motion is the reduction of something from potentiality to actuality, and such a reduction can only be made by something in actuality. A thing cannot be in act and potency at the same time and in the same respect. Consequently, a thing cannot be the cause of its own motion, but must be moved by something else, which in turn is moved by another, and that by another, and so on. However, to explain motion it is necessary that we

[34] *Summa Contra Gentiles*, Bk. I, Chap. 11.
[35] *Ibid.*, Chap. 12. Cf. *Summa Theologica*, 2, Art. 2.
[36] *Summa Theologica*, 2, Art. 2, Reply obj. 1.

go back to a first cause of motion which is itself unmoved, for it is impossible to proceed to infinity.[37]

Thomas' proof depends upon two premises which he believes have been substantiated by Aristotle: everything moved is moved by another, and with regard to things which are the cause of motion and things moved one cannot proceed to infinity.[38]

If a thing were itself the cause of its own motion, it would be moved immediately, so that when one of its parts is at rest the whole is at rest. If one part were at rest and the other in motion, the whole thing would not be moved immediately, but only that part which is moved while the other is at rest. But if the rest of one thing depends on the rest of another, its movement also depends on the movement of another. Consequently, what is moved is moved by another.[39]

Moreover, whatever is moved by accident is not self-moved, for its movement depends on the motion of another.[40] And nothing is in potency and act in the same respect and at the same time, and since whatever causes motion is in act, and since what is moved is in potency, therefore, nothing is mover and moved, so nothing is the cause of its own motion.[41]

The second proposition that Thomas holds with Aristotle, is that there can be no procession to infinity in the series of movers and things moved, for every body that causes something to be in motion is itself moved. And if it were possible to go back to infinity, an infinite number of bodies would be in motion in a finite time.[42] Secondly, in an ordered series of movers and things moved, if the first cause of motion is taken away, intermediate causes of motion will cease to cause motion and motion will cease.[43] Moreover, by removing the first mover,

[37] *Ibid.*, Art. 3.
[38] *Summa Contra Gentiles*, Bk. I, Chap. 13 (3) (4).
[39] *Ibid.*, Bk. I, Chap. 13, pp. 5, 6. See also Gilson, *The Christian Philosophy of St. Thomas Aquinas*, pp. 60 ff.
[40] *Summa Contra Gentiles*, Bk. I, Chap. 13, p. 8.
[41] *Ibid.*, (9).
[42] *Ibid.*, (12). Cf. Gilson, *Chrisitian Philosophy of St. Thomas Aquinas*, pp. 61-62.
[43] *Summa Contra Gentiles*, Bk. I, Chap. 13 (14).

only instrumental moving causes will exist, and no principal moving cause, but the former cannot exist without the latter, and nothing will be in motion.[44]

The existence of a first unmoved mover can also be shown by showing that the proposition "every mover is moved" is not true by itself or by accident.[45] For if whatever is the cause of motion is moved, is accidentally true, then it is not necessary and the possibility exists that none of the things that are in motion are moved, so that there may be no motion. The unacceptability of this conclusion demonstrates, however, that the proposition whatever is the cause of motion is moved by another is not accidentally true.[46]

Moreover, if it is true in itself that every mover is moved, a further difficulty would arise, namely, the same thing would be possessed and not possessed by the same being. If, however, the mover is moved by another species of motion, we cannot proceed to infinity since the genera and species of movement are finite in number, and a first mover will exist which is itself not moved.

But even granted that a first mover is not moved by an exterior cause, the first mover may not be absolutely unmoved, since it might be self-moved. However, since the same being cannot be in potency and act at the same time and under the same relation, only one part of the self-moved mover can be moving and the other part solely moved.[47]

God is not a part of a self-moving mover. Everything moving itself is moved through desire of an object higher in the order of motion, than the mover desiring it. Above the mover that moves by desire is the object causing its desire. The supreme desirable, God, is the first cause of all movement. The notion of an unmovable mover is identical with the notion of God. "Therefore, it is necessary to arrive at a first mover, moved by no other; and this everyone understands to be God."[48] A com-

---

[44] *Ibid.,* (15).

[45] Cf. Gilson, *loc. cit.,* pp. 62 ff., and *Summa Contra Gentiles,* Bk. I, Chap. 13, para. 17, 18, 19.

[46] *Summa Contra Gentiles,* Bk. I, Chap. 13, para. 17. Cf. Gilson, *loc. cit.,* p. 62.

[47] *Summa Contra Gentiles,* Bk. I, Chap. 13, para. 21-23.

[48] *Summa Theologica,* Q. 2, Art. 3, obj. 2.

plete demonstration of this identity is, however, apparent when it is subsequently shown that the divine attributes accessible to reason are deducible from the notion of a first unmovable mover.

Thomas has not sought to show that present motion requires a prime cause in the past, but that actually given motion is unintelligible without a first mover. The structure of the proof does not change, therefore, even if the eternity of the world is accepted. That the world had a beginning in time is not subject to demonstration.[49]

Thomas' first proof for the existence of God thus borrows nothing from revelation. It simply considers a hierarchically ordered series of causes. For whatever is moved in the physical universe is moved by a moving cause superior to it, and each particular moving cause, within the species, cannot be the primary source of its motion, so that the sufficient reason for the efficiency of individuals must be sought outside of the species. And whatever acts in virtue of a received nature is only an instrumental cause which is ultimately related to a first cause.

St. Thomas' second way to God is based on the nature of efficient cause. The physical world presents an order of efficient causes in which no thing is the efficient cause of itself, since such would necessitate that a thing be prior to itself. Nor can there be an infinity of efficient causes, since in their order, the first is the cause of the intermediate, and the latter the cause of the last cause. And the removal of the cause implies the removal of the effect so that the absence of a first efficient cause would imply the absence of an intermediate and last cause. And if it were possible to go on to infinity there would be no first efficient cause, so that it is necessary to admit a first efficient cause which is God.[50]

The necessity of a first cause is here again based on the impossibility of going back to infinity, but whereas the first way to God discloses that he is the cause of cosmic motion, the

[49] *Summa Contra Gentiles*, Bk. I, Chap. 13 (30).
[50] *Summa Theologica*, Q. 2, Art. 3, obj. 2; and *Summa Contra Gentiles*, Bk. I, Chap. 13, para. 33.

second makes him the cause of the existence of things, the cause of being, and thereby discloses a different aspect of divine causality.[51]

The third way to God discloses that the God known as the moving and efficient cause is also necessary being. It is based upon the fact that in nature things are possible to be and not to be. But if there is nothing that is not necessary, at one time nothing was in existence, and nothing would now exist, so that the existence of a necessary being, God, must be posited.[52] In other words, the possible is contingent and does not have its existence from itself.

The fourth way to God proceeds from an examination of the degrees of being. For in things we find a gradation. Some are more and some less good, and *more* or *less* are predicated of things according as they resemble a maximum, and the latter in any genus is the cause of all in that genus, so that there must be something which is to all beings, the cause of their perfection: God.[53] In other words, whatever does not possess a perfection of itself and completely, possesses it because of something possessing it of itself and in the highest degree. And the very intelligibility of the perfection of things arises from their resemblance to God.[54]

The fifth way to God is based on the notion of final cause. Natural bodies lack knowledge but act nevertheless for an end, since they always or nearly always act in the same way to obtain the best result. And that they achieve their end by design is explicable on the hypothesis that some intelligent being exists which directs them to their end, and this being is called God.[55]

Thus, each of Thomas' proofs of the existence of God is purportedly based on the observation of an empirical fact; that there is motion, reciprocal action in things, beings that are born and die, more or less perfect things, and that there

[51] Gilson, *The Christian Philolosphy of St. Thomas Aquinas*, p. 67.
[52] *Summa Theologica*, 2, Art. 3.
[53] *Idem.*
[54] Gilson, *loc. cit.*, p. 74.
[55] *Summa Theologica*, Q. 2, Art. 2.

is order in things. Each employs causal inference by showing that God is the sole cause of sensible experience, and each supposes that the effects with which it deals are arranged in a series of more or less perfect causes which makes an infinite regression impossible. The sufficient reason of existence of any single existence supposedly proves the existence of God without the aid of faith or revelation,[56] and the Thomistic proofs supposedly reach beyond existences which are not self-sufficient to a self-sufficient existence, which is the first cause of all other existences; to *Him Who Is.*

Thus theology and philosophy may on occasion approach God in different ways, but the existence of God is known properly to philosophy by reason alone. Consequently, a demonstration of the existence of God by philosophy is at the same time a demonstration of the harmony of philosophy and theology, even though certain other truths about God are known solely to revelation.

The present-day Thomist, in following St. Thomas, does not maintain that a scientific demonstration of God's existence can be given in the sense that such a demonstration does not go beyond the data of observation. Rather, he holds that reason itself requires that we recognize that sense phenomena cannot explain themselves but require the presence of a cause which makes them intelligible, a cause which can be found solely beyond observation on the scientific level, on the higher level of philosophical or metaphysical explanation.[57]

The positive sciences do not give the *raison d'etre* of things. The principle of causality employed by neo-Thomism to attain to knowledge of God rests on the alleged self-evident principle that everything which is has a sufficient reason for existing.[58] Knowledge of God is natural in that it belongs to the rational order, not to the supernatural order of faith.[59] And it is natural

[56] Gilson, *loc. cit.*, pp. 76-77.

[57] R. Garrigou-Lagrange, *God, His Existence and His Nature*, Vol. I (St. Louis: B. Herder Book Co., 1948), pp. 62 ff.

[58] *Ibid.*, p. 181.

[59] Jacques Maritain, *Approaches to God* (New York: Harper Brothers, 1954), p. 2.

in that in man there is a pre-philosophical, instinctive awareness of God, awakened in man by the awareness of his own finite
existence and the existence of being. In this primordial intuition
of being which does not exist by virtue of itself man becomes
aware of self-subsisting Being existing through itself, and is
confronted with the existence of God.[60]

The proofs of Thomas are for Maritain the development, the
unfolding of our natural knowledge, raised to the level of
metaphysical certitude.[61] The philosophical proofs of the existence of God are, however, justifiable solely on a philosophical
level. And it is on such a level that the philosopher realizes
that the intellect differs by nature from the senses, and is able
to attain knowledge of Being in things,[62] even on levels which
cannot be touched by the senses. The philosopher ought to know
that the laws of being, the principle of identity, every being is
what it is, is valid of all being, and that the principle of causality,
applies to all contingent being. For everything that is contingent
has a cause, and is intelligible through another thing.

The principle of causality on which Thomas' ways to God are
based is known by an immediate intellectual intuition; it
reaches beyond the contingent world of experience, and seeks
the *raisons d'etre* demanded by things because they are contingent. And it is partly because of this principle that Thomas'
ways to God are valid today.[63]

The formal principle of the five ways, the necessity of a first
cause, which is subsistent in its own right, is the same in each,
but each proof is, nevertheless, distinct in that it rests on distinct data of experience.

Maritain agrees with Thomas that there is no contradiction
in the idea of an infinite multitude or of a succession without
beginning or end. For there is no contradiction in assuming an
infinite series of homogeneous causes on the same level, each
accounting for the following one in existence.

[60] *Ibid.*, pp. 4 ff.
[61] *Ibid.*, p. 11.
[62] *Ibid.*, p. 20.
[63] *Ibid.*, pp. 21-23.

But the causes to which Thomas' ways refer do not merely disclose a temporal succession, but are logically superordinated to each other in the order of intelligible conditioning. They are causes on different levels, each accounts for the nature or determination in being of the following, and thereby accounts for its very *raison d'etre*. The line of intelligible conditioning leads vertically to a transcendent cause, infinitely different in nature.[64]

The first cause established by the five "ways" is characterized as God by his essential distinction from other beings and by his infinite transcendence, although, subsequent argument and analysis is needed to establish further propositions about his nature.

Maritain is not unaware of Kant's contention that the concept of an absolutely necessary being, as a concept of pure reason, does not have objective reality because it is required by reason. The unconditioned necessity of judgments is not identical with the necessity of things.[65] The existence of an absolutely necessary being can be rejected without contradiction. It is therefore illegitimate to introduce the concept of existence into the concept of a thing. For all existential propositions are synthetic.[66]

The concept of a supreme being is not able to enlarge our knowledge about what exists. For the fact of existence adds nothing to a concept. And the criterion of the possibility of synthetic knowledge can be found in experience alone.[67] Therefore the fact that we cannot conceive of God except as existing in no way insures his actual existence.

Kant does not simply reject the ontological argument, but holds that the cosmological argument is equally deceptive,[68] since it reasons from the unconditioned necessity of some

---

[64] *Ibid.*, p. 40.
[65] Immanuel Kant, *Critique of Pure Reason*, trans. Norman Kemp Smith (New York: MacMillan and Co., 1943), pp. 500 ff.
[66] *Ibid.*, p. 504.
[67] *Ibid.*, p. 507.
[68] *Ibid.*, p. 510.

being to the unlimited reality of that being. The cosmological argument holds that if anything exists, an absolutely necessary being also exists, and since at least I exist, the desired conclusion is reached.

Experience is in fact used by the cosmological proof only to conclude to the existence of a supreme being, the properties of which cannot be determined by experience, so that in effect the cosmological proof presupposes the ontological proof. Otherwise it could not infer that the concept of an *ens realissimum* is the only concept appropriate and adequate to necessary existence. Experience is unable to demonstrate that absolute necessity belongs to any determinate thing.[69]

Moreover, the proposition that every necessary being is the most real of all beings when converted implies that every *ens realissimum* is a necessary being. And such is determined solely from the fact that the concept of *ens realissimum* implies its absolute necessity, which could be the case only if the ontological proof were valid, an assertion not admitted by the cosmological argument.[70]

The contingent can have meaning solely in the sensible world, and the principle of causality is meaningless when extended beyond the latter. And even within the world of experience there is no justification for the assertion that the impossibility of an infinite series of causes implies a first cause. It is illegitimate, on the ground that we can think of nothing further, to remove all conditions which make the concept of necessity possible and then complete the concept of the series. The cosmological proof confuses logical possibility with actuality.[71]

The existence of an all-sufficient being can be postulated as an admissible hypothesis, but it cannot be said with absolute certainty that such a being necessarily exists.[72] The ideal of a supreme being is only a regulative principle of reason. And the

[69] *Ibid.*, p. 511.
[70] *Ibid.*, p. 512.
[71] *Ibid.*, p. 513.
[72] *Ibid.*, p. 517.

concept of necessity is a formal condition of thought, not a material condition of existence.

The only other possible rational demonstration of the existence of God, can also, according to Kant, be shown to be unsatisfactory. Such an alleged proof, designated by the term "physico-theological," proceeds on the basis of a determinate experience of the constitution and order of things within the world to a supreme being. But the very idea of a necessary and all-sufficient being is so far above anything empirical, that the latter can never be expected to provide a sufficient basis for such an inference.

All laws pertaining to cause and effect, all synthesis and extension of our knowledge refer to possible experience, to objects of the sensible world. Consequently reason is unable to bridge the gap between a series of natural causes and a transcendent intelligible being.

The physico-theological proof is based on our experience of order in accord with a determinate purpose believed to be alien to the things themselves, so that such order is explicable in terms of an intelligent cause, the unity of which can be inferred from the unity of the real reciprocal relations existing between the parts of the world. Thus the order and purposiveness of the world presupposes the existence of a cause proportional to it, a being possessing all the perfection proper to an all sufficient being.

The difficulty is, however, that physico-theology is unable to give any determinate concept of the supreme cause of the world, since empirical analysis can never lead to an absolute totality beyond the sensible world, so that the gap can only be filled by the ontological argument.

Now in spite of Kant's criticism, Maritain still believes it possible to follow Thomas' paths to God, since an erroneous theory of existence is involved in Kant's view of a concept and a judgment. Kant was correct in pointing out the weakness of the ontological argument. A purely analytical process cannot reach existence itself without presupposing any datum of experience. But Kant wrongly concluded that the concept of existence adds nothing to a subject and is not a predicate.[75] Existence has a content, an intelligible value. It is a predicate with reference to a perfection, the actuality of every act.[76]

When reason establishes the existence of God, it starts with data of experience where existence is apprehended, and under the compulsion of intuitively grasped first principles it compounds the notion of a first supreme cause with that of existence, so that reason does not need to employ the ontological argument, for reason knows the existence of a first cause from experience itself.[77]

Kant fails to see the radical difference between conception and assertion, between simple apprehension and judgment.[78]

According to Maritain, Kant argued that to demonstrate the existence of God by his effects is to establish the existence of an absolutely necessary being, starting from contingent existence, and to conclude that such a being is God, since the absolutely necessary being is supremely perfect. The ontological argument is thus presupposed by the cosmological argument, since the proposition "the absolutely necessary being is supremely perfect" is the major premise of the ontological argument "the supremely perfect being is absolutely necessary." But Maritain raises the question as to what constitutes the heart of the ontological argument. Does it identify necessary existence and supreme perfection, or does it pass from supreme perfection conceived to necessary existence affirmed?[79]

If the two theses—"any supremely perfect being is absolutely necessary" and "any absolutely necessary being is supremely perfect"—are taken as equivalent, the first holds that "any supremely perfect being merely represented exists necessarily in

[75] Jacques Maritain, *The Dream of Descartes* (New York: Philosophical Library, 1944), pp. 135 ff.
[76] *Ibid.*, p. 136.
[77] *Ibid.*, p. 137.
[78] *Ibid.*, p. 138.
[79] *Ibid.*, pp. 139 ff.

effect," and the second holds that "any absolutely necessary being merely represented exists effectively with complete perfection." But it is exactly this line of reasoning that Maritain refuses to follow. For he would begin by establishing that an absolutely necessary being exists, and he then feels justified in concluding that this being, of which he knows that it exists, possesses a supreme perfection which also exists.

The pitfalls of the ontological argument are avoided if one merely affirms that if it exists, every supremely perfect being exists with an absolute necessity, or if it exists, any absolutely necessary being is supremely perfect. Thomas does not begin with a concept but with experience. He first establishes the existence of a primary cause or intelligence, and it is only after the question of existence has been decided that he concludes that such a being is pure act and infinite perfection. Thus, Thomas does not pass from the ideal to the real, but from the real to the real.[80]

The Principle of Causality

Maritain contends that Kant erroneously defines causality as a functioning of phenomena, whereas causality is properly related to being, and it implies the realization of that which is without being.[81] The deity is, however, above what circumscribes the idea of being.[82] The divine essence is attained and known in things which resemble and differ from it.[83] The notion of causality employed to demonstrate the existence of God functions by reason of the nature of being and thus transcends the limits of time and space imposed by Kant.[84] Cause is a primary notion of being which analogically denotes an analogical perfection of an absolutely perfect Being. To be the cause of a being is to bring it into existence, to actualize it.[85] And it is be-

---

[80] Cf. Garrigou-Lagrange, *op. cit.*, p. 208.
[81] Maritain, *The Degrees of Knowledge*, pp. 262 ff.
[82] *Ibid.*, p. 284.
[83] Garrigou-Lagrange, *op. cit.*, p. 209.
[84] *Ibid.*, p. 300.
[85] Maritain, *The Degrees of Knowledge*, pp. 94 ff.

cause the proofs of the existence of God are based upon a basic principle of being that they are not subject to Kant's critique.

The proofs of the existence of God presuppose a critical realism, an Aristotelian-Thomist conception of knowledge. The critical problem is not how is it possible to pass from *percepi* to *esse* for the intellect deals first of all with being, and it discovers the principle of identity in its very apprehension of it. Epistemology is itself a part of metaphysics, and it has no existence apart from the latter; consequently Kant is unable to refute the Thomistic proofs of the existence of God by means of an epistemological analysis of pure phenomena. For it suffices for things to exist independently of the mind for God to become inevitable.[86]

God is known to the metaphysician, not by what He is in himself but by analogy, via transcendental perfections found in Him and in things.[87] Man's knowledge of God by ideas and concepts, although true, is nevertheless deficient.[88] The mind is able to consider abstract objects from which matter has been eliminated; it can attain knowledge of being as being, but the essence of God is not therefore fully known.

It is because we can have metaphysical knowledge that the existence of God can be known. Before knowing that John is human, one knows he is a being. Being is thus an intelligible object, a transcendental object of thought.[89]

The principle of identity—A is A—is not simply a logical principle but is also an ontological principle, which when transferred into the logical order, becomes the first law of mind. And what is true of the principle of identity is also true of the principle of causality employed to prove God's existence.

The principle of causality is known by an intuition bearing on the primary aspects of being, although it may be provoked in the mind by a sensible example. It is a metaphyical axiom of

[86] *Ibid.*, p. 8.
[87] *Ibid.*, p. 17.
[88] *Ibid.*, pp. 258 ff.
[89] *Ibid.*, p. 264.

which every philosopher ought immediately to be aware, an axiom which reasoning itself presupposes.

The principle of causality is intellectually seen. It imposes itself with absolute necessity, by force of the notion of being itself. It is rooted in the intelligible, not in sensible appearances.[90]

The principle of causality, as a metaphysical principle, belongs to a perfect form of knowledge. It is a part of a true science. It belongs to the world of the supra-universal, to a sphere of intelligibility having its determination in itself.[91] Thus metaphysics reaches above time, and grasps a world of eternal truths, a world which does not need the verification of the senses.[92]

The principle of causality by which God is known does not arise from an analysis of the sensible but from necessities which are intuitively grasped in being. When given a diversity of things which do not suffice for their own existence, we know immediately that they depend upon a cause sufficient for their existence.

The principle of causality is therefore pregnant with ontological meaning. It is an ontological principle which is not derived from experience, but which applies to the latter.[93]

The principle of causality may be dispensed with in the sphere of phenomena, but it is indispensible in the sphere of being. For as soon as the existence of a contingent being is admitted, the existence of necessary being is implied.[94] Thus a philosopher cannot think of the non-sufficiency of his thought without knowing that it depends on supra-thought. An infinite series is impossible here since it is a reason of being which is here sought, and an infinite series is not a reason of being.[95] My act of thought is caused by an absolute uncaused thought. And it is after I know that such a thought is an existing reality that

[90] *Ibid.*, p. 267.
[91] *Ibid.*, p. 268.
[92] *Ibid.*, p. 274.
[93] Cf. E. L. Mascall, *He Who Is* (London: Longmans, Green and Co., 1943), p. 68.
[94] Maritain, *The Degrees of Knowledge*, p. 275.
[95] *Ibid.*, p. 276.

I deduce his infinite perfections. Real existence is not here deduced from the idea of total perfection. But without recourse to the ontological argument, it is known that being *a se* exists, and that the notion of aseity includes total perfection.[96]

To demonstrate the existence of God is, however, not to subject him to our grasp. The concepts and names which describe God's perfections, although fully realized in God, do not delimit divine reality.[97] The divine perfections are identical in God, and the deity is above everything which circumscribes the idea of being.[98] And yet metaphysics demonstrably knows in a manner which will become evident, that the divine essence subsists in itself.[99]

The Attributes of God

The neo-Thomist is not satisfied to demonstrate the existence of a first cause which is an immanent principle of the world. If philosophy is to be able to prove the existence of the "true God," it must be able to demonstrate that certain attributes belong to the first cause.

Philosophy is not able to disclose the immensity of the divine substance, since the latter surpasses the intellect. We are unable to apprehend the essence of God by knowing what it is, and yet we are able to have some knowledge of it by knowing what it is not.[100]

The manner of God's existence can be ascertained by considering "how he is not," i.e.,[101] by removing from him whatever is not proper to him. The divine attributes can be deduced, since God is self-subsisting being,[102] a fact which implies a real distinction between God and the world, and, therefore, permits the removal of composition and thereby establishes his simplicity via negation.

---

[96] *Ibid.*, p. 278.
[97] *Ibid.*, pp. 280 ff.
[98] *Ibid.*, p. 288.
[99] Maritain, *The Dream of Descartes*, p. 64.
[100] *Summa Theologica*, Q. III, 1st Art.
[101] Garrigou-Lagrange, *op. cit.*, pp. 56 ff.
[102] *Summa Theologica*, Q. III, 1st Art.

Whatever is not compatible with the pure actuality of being cannot pertain to the notion of God. Therefore, he is not a body, first of all, since a body only moves when it is moved, and the proofs of his existence demonstrate that the first mover is unmoved. And, secondly since every body is in potentiality of which God is devoid, God is not a body. And finally, the fact that God is the most noble of things, and that the body is less noble than the soul, on which it depends for animation, again warrants the conclusion that God is not a body.[103]

As an attribute, the simplicity of God applies analogically to God, and as an attribute, it is formally in God. Matter is excluded from God, since matter exists in potentiality and God is pure act. Everything composed of matter and form is a participated good, whereas God is the essential good, as was shown in the fourth proof of his existence; consequently, God cannot be composed of matter and form.[104]

God is the same as his essence or nature, since such identity holds of things not composed of matter and form. God is his deity. God and the Godhead are identical. And there cannot be any distinction in God between his essence and substance.[105]

God is really and essentially distinct from every finite being in that God and only God is his existence. Essence and being are identical in God. A thing which differs from its essence is caused by another, but the proofs of God's existence show that God is the first efficient cause, so that it is impossible that in God his being should not be identical with his essence. Secondly, since God is pure act, and in him there is no potentiality, his essence is not potentiality for existence, but is existence. And finally, since God is the first Being, he is essential being, and essential being is its own existence.

God is not in any genus, since nothing is prior to God in meaning or in reality, and genus is prior in meaning to what

---

[103] *Ibid.*, 2nd Art.

[104] *Ibid.*, Art. 3. Cf. Garrigou-Lagrange, *op. cit.*, pp. 177 ff, and E. Gilson, *The Christian Philosophy of St. Thomas Aquinas*, p. 88.

[105] *Summa Theologica*, q. 3, Art. 5, and *Summa Contra Gentiles*, Bk. 1, Chap. 25.

it contains.[106] Nor can there be any accident in God, since God is without potentiality, and God is his own being, and what is essential is prior to what is accidental.[107] God is, therefore, absolutely simple,[108] for he is the first being, the first cause, pure act, and self-subsisting being. All composition is thus excluded from him.[109] Nor does God enter into the composition of other things.[110]

Reason is able to establish God's simplicity by proving that he is not composite. And this rational "truth" is in agreement with what has been revealed of God in Exodus III, 13-15, where God is portrayed as "He who is," or as self-subsisting being.

To the attribute of divine simplicity a second can be added: the divine perfection. It is not possible to conceive of a perfect being, but we can affirm the perfection of God by denying all imperfection to him. The nature of God's perfection is beyond reason, but that he is perfect is accessible to reason. By eliminating all possible imperfections, all conceivable perfection is attributed to God.[111]

The perfections predicated of God and of creatures denote things essentially different between which there is a certain proportion or analogy.[112]

There is no real or formal distinction between the divine attributes within the being of God. The distinction between simplicity and perfection actually only exists in the human mind. Supernatural revelation is needed to arrive at knowledge of God's essence as it is in itself, but we are still able to proceed in our understanding of the divine attributes as they are distinct from one another in our mode of knowing them, and we can find a certain order among them.[113] The fourth proof of God's existence, based on the degrees of being, makes it clear that

[106] *Summa Theologica*, q. 3, Art. 6.
[107] *Ibid.*, Art. 7.
[108] Garrigou-Lagrange, *op. cit.*, p. 191.
[109] *Summa Theologica*, q. 3, Art. 8.
[110] Gilson, *The Christian Philosophy of St. Thomas Aquinas*, p. 94.
[111] *Summa Theologica*, Q. 13, Art. 5.
[112] Garrigou-Lagrange, *op. cit.*, Vol. II, p. 9.
[113] *Ibid.*, p. 19.

God is Being-itself, and is, therefore, not subject to any limitations imposed on being by space or matter.[114] Self-subsisting being is what formally constitutes the divine nature as it is imperfectly known by us. The divine attributes which we imperfectly know are absolutely simple perfections which exist necessarily in God, and which we are able to deduce from what we conceive as constituting God's essence.[115]

In affirming that God is perfect, we deny all imperfection to God. As the first principle in the order of efficient cause, God is free of potentiality, and since perfect in proportion to his actuality, he lacks nothing of the mode of his perfection.[116] All the perfections of all things are in God, for whatever perfection exists in an effect must pre-exist in an agent, and the perfections of all created things are included in the perfection of being.[117] Consequently, the universality of God's perfection is demonstrable from the fact that God is the first effective cause of all things and because he is self-subsisting being.[118] Creatures can be like God in so far as they are beings, and in so far as God is the first principle of being.[119]

Thus, the supposition of a pure act-of-being, enables one to infer that a pure act-of-being is absolute perfection, since perfection is a certain way of being. God, who, in his act of being, is the pure being who lacks no perfection, has no defects.

Moreover, since perfection is to lack no good, to be perfect is to be the good, and God, as pure actuality of being, is therefore Good.[120] Goodness is identical with being,[121] although in idea, being is prior to goodness.[122] As being, every being is

---

[114] *Ibid.*, p. 33.

[115] *Summa Theologica*, Q. 4, Art. 1.

[116] *Ibid.*, Q. 4, Art. 2.

[117] R. Garrigou-Lagrange, *The One God* (London: B. Herder Co., 1946), p. 207.

[118] *Summa Theologica*, Q. 4, Art. 3, and *Summa Contra Gentiles*, Bk. 1, Chap. 29.

[119] Gilson, *loc. cit.*, pp. 98 ff.

[120] *Summa Theologica*, Q. 5, Art. 1.

[121] *Ibid.*, Art. 2.

[122] *Ibid.*, Art. 4.

good.[123] Goodness is not a supplementary quality which is added to God's being. "To be is to be good."[124] For God to be good and for God to exist is the same thing. God alone is essentially good, since only in God is essence identical with his being.

And to affirm that God is perfect and that he is absolutely good is to affirm his infinity, since God is his own subsistent being, and is not a being received in anything. Infinity is a mode of perfection of the divine nature and of every attribute.[125]

Since God is infinite, he is present in all things, not in essence, but as an agent is present to that upon which he acts. Nothing is foreign or exterior to God as a limit to his existence. To hold that there is nothing in which God is not present is to affirm his omnipresence. God is the cause of the being of creatures, not only at their creation, but throughout their duration. "God is the act-of-being of all that exists, not in this sense that He is their essence, but in that He is their cause. . . ."

God is the act of existing of whatever exists. He is in all things by his *Esse* causing their *esse*.[126]

Thus philosophy and theology follow a dual path to the same truth. The existence and the attributes of God, known by reason, agree with the knowledge of God disclosed in revelation, and with the mysteries of faith.

Nevertheless, the harmony between the knowledge of natural reason and the knowledge of grace does not imply that natural reason imposes a limit upon our knowledge of God. Philosophy knows that God is, and that he is one. Philosophy is able to express many negative judgments concerning God by speaking of how God is not; but there is also a knowledge of God beyond philosophical knowledge, a knowledge beyond human understanding.

Grace supplies man with a more perfect knowledge of God than does the natural reason of philosophy. The latter requires images derived from sensible things and an intelligible light

[123] Gilson, *loc. cit.*, p. 98.
[124] *Summa Theologica*, Q. 6, Art. 1.
[125] Gilson, *loc. cit.*, p. 102.
[126] *Summa Theologica*, Q. 3, Art. 4.

which permits abstract intelligible conceptions to be abstracted from them.[127] The natural light of reason is strengthened by the infusion of grace, the light of faith. Faith is a sort of knowledge, but it is not a knowledge determined by the understanding of first principles. Faith determines the intellect to an object which is not naturally knowable. God's revelation provides the believer, for example, with the truth that the Deity consists of three persons, and thus he is known more fully. But our rational knowledge is based exclusively upon sensible effects which do not fully express the power of the first cause. Such effects enable us to reach the conclusion that God exists, and that the lack of certain perfections would make it impossible for him to be the first cause,[128] but they do not enable us to arrive at the pure being of God, and achieve positive knowledge of God.[129]

The complete power of God cannot be known from the knowledge of sensible things, nor can God's essence be seen. We know what necessarily belongs to God as the first cause, and we know his relationship to his effects, but knowledge of his essence is open only to the good, and is by grace.[130]

Is it then impossible for philosophy to know anything more about God than what he is not? The problem concerns the degree of resemblance to God that can be attributed to his effects.[131] In attributing perfection to God the assumption is made that the first cause possesses the perfections found in creatures to an eminent degree, but the way in which such perfections belong to God eludes us.[132]

In the case of an equivocal cause, the order of its perfection transcends its effect.[133] The effects of God are not one with God in nature or in name, but are greatly inferior to him. As an equivocal cause God contains the effects he creates so that their

---

[127] *Ibid*, Q. 12, Art. 12.
[128] Gilson, *loc. cit.*, p. 104.
[129] *Ibid*.
[130] *Summa Contra Gentiles*, I, 29.
[131] *Ibid*, 32.
[132] *Ibid.*, Chap. 34.
[133] *Summa Theologica*, Q. 13, Art. 5.

perfections are attributable to him, but the manner in which they are in him is unknown. In him the perfections attributed to him are what he is and as he is. "Nothing can be predicated univocally of God and other things."[134] The effects of God receive in a divided and particular way what in God is simple and universal. And nothing is in God which is not divine being itself. Nevertheless, all the names applied to God and creatures are not, therefore, purely equivocal. That the names applied to God and creatures are related as cause and effect suggests a mean between the equivocal and the univocal: the notion of analogy.

Analogy or proportion can occur when several things are related to one other thing in different ways, or it can occur when one thing is bound to another because of a uniting relationship. And it is this latter form of analogy which enables some things to be said of God and creatures analogically.

Hence, whatever is said of God and creatures is said according as there is some relation of the creature to God as to principle and cause, wherein all the perfections of things pre-exist excellently.[135]

The perfections that we ascribe to God are in God, since God is their cause. When something has a positive perfection, God is that positive perfection, as the effect is in its cause.

The most proper name of God is "He who is," because it is the principal of all names applied to God. For the divine attributes when taken individually are not in God as a distinct reality. "And since we can in no way conceive of an essence which is only an act of being, we can in no way conceive of what God is, even with the help of such attributes."[136]

Thus Gilson writes:

The concept which we form of this effect cannot at all be transformed for us into the concept of God which we lack. But we can attribute to God, by an affirmative judgment, the name which designates the perfection corresponding to this effect. This procedure does

[134] *Ibid.*
[135] Gilson, *loc. cit.*, p. 107.
[136] *Summa Theologica*, Q. 13, Art. 12.

not affirm that God is like the creature. It is based on the certitude that, since every effect resembles its cause, the creature with which we start certainly resembles God. So we attribute to God several names, such as good, intelligent or wise; and these names are not synonyms, since each of them designates our distinct concept of a distinct, created being. Nevertheless, this multiplicity of names designates a simple object, because we attribute all of them to the same object by way of judgment.[137]

Our knowledge of God consists in our ability to form affirmative propositions about him. The contention that true positive statements can be made about God does not pertain solely to statements the truth of which is based on faith. But reason itself knows that such affirmative propositions can be made.

The intellect knows God under diverse conceptions since it cannot see him as he is in himself, but it knows that an identical reality corresponds to its diverse conceptions.

The fact that goodness, intelligence, and power, for example, do not exist, as such, as definite forms in the divine being, does not imply that nothing positive is affirmed, when it is said that 'God is good.' What is affirmed is the divine substance itself.

By saying that 'God is good,' more is said than that 'God is not bad.'

"So when we say, 'God is good,' the meaning is not, God is the cause of goodness, or, God is not evil; but the meaning is, whatever good we attribute to creatures pre-exists in God and in a higher way. Hence it does not follow that God is good because he causes goodness; but rather on the contrary, He causes goodness in things because He is good."[137a]

Philosophy agrees with the theology in that it is able to know that the proposition "God exists," is a true proposition. But philosophy does not know what God's act-of-being is in itself: God's existence is the same as his substance, and as his substance is unknown so also his existence. It is possible for philoso-

[137] Gilson, *loc. cit.*, p. 109.
[137a] *Idem.*

phy to show what the divine attributes are, but it is not possible to state what God is. Nevertheless, Gilson agrees with Thomas when Gilson writes:

> But in spite of all this, we are quite sure that even as the proposition "God exists" is true, so the propositions "God is good," "God is life," "God is intelligent," and others of the same kind, are also true. That God is what we call goodness, life and will we know as surely as we know that He is what we call being. But the meaning of these terms does not change when we apply them to God. All these judgments direct our understanding toward the same goal, the direction of which is known to us but which, because it is at infinity, is beyond the reach of our natural forces. For we do not attain it by multiplying the affirmative propositions which denote it. But yet to make these propositions is neither to waste our words nor our efforts, because it is at least to turn ourselves toward Him.[138]

Metaphysical knowledge of God utilizes, in the manner set forth, notions found in things and applies such to God without limitation or imperfection. It presupposes at the outset that the human intelligence is in no way limited to the sensory, but is rather ordinated to the perception of being concretized in sensible things, and is able to draw from material things, a conceptual object beyond the visible, and thus to conceive of being freed from sensory limitations; and in the realm of being it is able to seek the reasons for the concrete manifestation of being. Human nature is thus able to ascend above the human, and to know God, not in his essence, but in such transcendental perfections which are analogically common to the divine and the created.[139]

Theology, the science of revealed mysteries, is above metaphysics, the wisdom of the natural order. Its special light is the disclosure of knowledge that God has of himself, made known to us by revelation. It is a wisdom of faith, not of reason, a faith which utilizes reason by employing human logic, but its roots are super-natural in that they exist by faith. Theology

[138] *Idem.*
[139] Maritain, *The Degrees of Knowledge*, p. 207.

rationally develops the truths of revelation; it is the science of God, and since it is reason illuminated by faith, its certitude is higher than that of metaphysics.

Theology knows God in the mystery of his essence, in his own being, in that which belongs to him alone. The God known to theology is inaccessible to reason alone, since the latter knows him as the first cause of the natural order, and discovers what he has in common analogically with other beings. And yet it is the same God that is known to reason and to faith, to philosophy and to theology. And in a sense philosophy knows the same God who is known face to face in the beatific vision, for in reality the God known to theology is the common object of the vision of the blessed.

Faith is the craving for the beatific vision. And faith meets metaphysics where the latter points toward the point where all the perfections of the created world converge.

Metaphysical knowledge grasps God as its object only to the degree that the latter condescends to reason. But faith comprehends God in a way that is above us, but which is still proportionate to our nature.

Theology elucidates the substance of revelation by a faith united with reason. It employs philosophy as its servant and is under no obligation to philosophy, but can choose such philosophical doctrines as serve its purpose.

Nevertheless, philosophy remains true to its own order and employs a strictly rational method; it finds its harmony with theology in the discovery of the same object: God, and in a conception of nature and reason, open to the supernatural.

II. The Neo-Augustinianism of Herman Dooyeweerd

Certain features of Augustine's philosophy have been especially influential on Dooyeweerd. Augustine's entire writings are permeated by a single desire: to know God and the human soul. By contemplating the realities of consciousness, the primary objects of contemplation, Augustine proceeded to contemplate the world. But his interest in the world was always subordinate to his desire to understand God. And his interest in philosophy was always subordinate to the authority of Christ which he regarded as superior to reason.[1] The true wisdom is not to be found in the wisdom of the ancients but in the true wisdom which is Christ. A true philosopher, a philosopher faithful to his profession, would recognize "Christ, the virtue of God and the wisdom of God, and would not, in the pride of vain science, have revolted from his wholesome humility."[2]

The certain knowledge sought by Augustine was not to be found in the writings of those who forbid

... belief in things unknown ... as all heretics do and they who in the superstition of the gentiles are called philosophers. Not that the

---

[1] Cf. Augustine, *The Confessions*, Vol. I of *Nicene and Post-Nicene Fathers of the Christian Church*, ed. Philip Schaff (1st series, 8 vols; New York: Scribner, 1881), Bk. 5, Chap., IV, p. 81.

[2] *Ibid.*, *The City of God*, Bk. 10, Chap. 28.

promise of knowledge is to be blamed; but because they deem the most healthful and necessary step of faith is to be neglected, by which we must needs ascend to something certain which nothing but that which is eternal can be. Hence it appears that they do not possess even this knowledge, which in contempt of faith they promise; seeing that they know not so useful and necessary a step thereof.[3]

Following the direction of Augustine, Anselm, Calvin and the entire Augustinian tradition assigned priority to faith instead of to reason. For Calvin wisdom consists of knowledge of God and of ourselves, and these two aspects of knowledge are so closely interwoven that it is difficult to determine whether knowledge of God is prior or subsequent to self-knowledge. For self-knowledge immediately involves the contemplation of God and vice versa.[4] Self-knowledge incites and assists in the search for God, and true knowledge of the self is precluded apart from knowledge of the divine character. The very idea of a deity is innately impressed on the mind of man,[5] yet ignorance and wickedness have partly extinguished the kind of knowledge that God requires, and even the structure of the world, which clearly displays God at every point, is useless to us because of our stupidity, so that revelation alone is sufficient to provide the sought after knowledge.[6]

Dooyeweerd is aware of his dependence on Calvin and Augustine, but he is not satisfied with the latter's failure to clarify the relation between philosophy and theology.[7] And Dooyeweerd regards his own position, which seeks to demonstrate the inner point of contact between religion and philoso-

---

[3] St. Augustine, *Expositions on the Book of Psalms.* Ps. VIII, 6, p. 29.

[4] John Calvin, *Institutes of the Christian Religion,* trans. by John Allen, Vol. I (7th American edition; Philadelphia: Presbyterian Board of Christian Education, 1936), pp. 47 ff.

[5] *Ibid.,* p. 56.

[6] *Ibid.,* p. 45 ff.

[7] Herman Dooyeweerd, *A New Critique of Theoretical Thought,* Vol. I, trans. David H. Freeman and William Young (Philadelphia: Presbyterian and Reformed Publishing Co., 1953), p. 178.

phy, as a recognition of the independence of philosophy, but of philosophy in a Christian form.[8]

Dooyeweerd does not object to Augustine's assigning priority to revelation and to faith, but unlike Augustine he would develop a Christian philosophy in which philosophical questions are not handled within the framework of an elaborately developed systematic theology. Dooyeweerd would subordinate philosophy to revelation (not to theology, in the scientific sense, since theology for Dooyeweerd, is itself subordinate to revelation), not because philosophy is arbitrarily thought to be the *ancilla theologiae,* but because a theoretical analysis of the nature of philosophical thought is able to disclose an essential unity between faith and reason. Thus while agreeing with Augustine in accepting the essential unity of the latter, Dooyeweerd goes beyond Augustine in seeking to present a philosophical demonstration of the intrinsic connection between faith and reason.

*A*ugustine's point of departure is, however, the basis of Dooyeweerd's alleged demonstration of the insufficieny of reason. For the reality of what Augustine calls the mind, and what Dooyeweerd refers to as the ego, is implicit in the very act of knowledge.[9] Doubt itself presupposes the existence of the mind. Nothing is more present to the mind than itself.[10] For Augustine, the mind knows with certainty that it is, that it understands, and that it lives.[11]

But since we treat of the nature of the mind, let us remove from our consideration all knowledge which is received from without, through the senses of the body; and attend more carefully to the position which we have laid down, that all minds know and are certain concerning themselves. . . . Yet who ever doubts that he him-

---

[8] *Ibid.,* p. 524.
[9] Cf. St. Augustine, *On the Trinity,* Vol. III of *Nicene and Post-Nicene Fathers of the Christian Church,* ed. Philip Schaff (1st series, 8 vols; New York: Scribner, 1888), IX, Chap. 6 and 7, and Dooyeweerd, *op. cit.,* p. 5. See further B. B. Warfield, *Studies in Tertullian and Augustine* (New York: Oxford University Press, 1930), pp. 138 ff.
[10] Augustine, *On the Trinity,* X, Chap. 3, p. 137.
[11] *Ibid.,* Bk. X, Chap. 10, p. 140.

self lives, and remembers, and understands, and wills and thinks, and knows, and judges; seeing that even if he doubts, he lives; if he doubts he remembers why he doubts. . . .[12]

Dooyeweerd follows Augustine's withdrawal from the external world, and seeks truth in the inner consciousness. Dooyeweerd's entire writings assume an immediate awareness of the ego, so that philosophy is thought to be impossible apart from critical self-reflection, without which even the external world is unintelligible. "Know thyself" must be rewritten above the portals of philosophy.[13]

Dooyeweerd's own conception of Christianity is essentially that of Augustine. The most basic motives of the Christian religion are thought by both to be that of creation, the fall into sin, and the redemption accomplished by Christ.

The exact theological significance of these motives is not always clearly stated by Dooyeweerd. But in an unspecified manner God is supposedly the origin of heaven and earth, so that there is no original power in opposition to God, and within the creation nothing is evident which gives expression to a dualistic principle of origin.[14]

The meaning of creation is expressed for Dooyeweerd in the 139th Psalm, in which the omniscience and omnipresence of the divine power is portrayed.[15] And the background of Dooyeweerd's motive of creation is readily found in the thought of Augustine who also held that God made all things in wisdom, and that nothing preceded creation.[16] For Augustine not only was the world created by God, but it was also created good, without any natural evil.[17] For all that, it owes its being to God and in God there is no evil.[18] God is not the progenitor

---

[12] *Ibid.*
[13] Dooyeweerd, *op. cit.*, p. 5.
[14] Dooyeweerd, *op. cit.*, p. 174 ff.
[15] Cf. Augustine, *Confessions*, Bk. I, Chap. 2.
[16] Augustine, *Tractate*, XXXVII, 8, pp. 216 ff.
[17] Augustine, *The City of God*, Bk. XL, Chap. 21, 22, 23.
[18] Augustine, *The Confessions*, Bk. VII, Chap. 40: 26.

of evil things.[19] Evil is simply a defect of the good. It is not nature but against nature.[20]

Dooyeweerd consciously embraces Augustine's emphasis on the absolute creative sovereignty of God, and his refusal to ascribe original power to evil.[21] He also follows Augustine in holding that Christ is the new religious root of the temporal cosmos.[22] For Augustine held that Christ had cosmic significance as the only begotten son of God, co-substantial and co-equal with the Father.[23] Christ is, therefore, the creator of all things,[24] and his acts are inseparable from those of the Father.[25] Christ has called us into existence, and has redeemed us,[26] and is thus the savior of the world.[27]

Dooyeweerd holds with Augustine that philosophy continues to be subject to error because of human sin.[29] But by belonging to Christ, the Christian is able to side with the kingdom of God, and check the activity of the kingdom of darkness. There is, therefore, in Dooyeweerd's thought an absolute antithesis with all philosophy which is not Christian philosophy.[30]

Christian philosophy in the past has, according to Dooyeweerd, always been a compromise philosophy, and in keeping with what he considers to be the true Augustinian spirit, Dooyeweerd would put an end to all synthesis between Christian and non-Christian thought. The cleft between faith and reason is thus thought to be a cleft between a Christian and a non-Christian conception of reason.[31]

---

[19] Augustine, *Acts or Disputation against Fortunatus*, 2nd Day.

[20] Augustine, *Against the Epistle of Manichaeus*, Chap. 35: 40.

[21] Dooeyweerd, *op. cit.*, p. 179. Cf. Herman Dooyeweerd, *Reformatie en Scholastiek in De Wysbegeerte*, Vol. I, T. Wever (Franeker, Netherlands: 1949), pp. 34 ff. See also *Philosophia Ref.*, 1936.

[22] Dooyeweerd, *A New Critique*, p. 506.

[23] Augustine, *Tractate XXIX*. Cf. *De Trinitate*, Bk. I, Chap. 5: 7.

[24] *Ibid.*, pp. 57 ff.

[25] Augustine, *Tractate*, XX, LXXI, CX.

[26] Augustine, *Tractate*, LI.

[27] Augustine, *Tractate XXXIV*.

[29] *New Critique*, I, p. 506. Cf. Augustine, *City of God*, Bk. XIX, Chap. 25.

[30] Cf. Augustine, *City of God*, Bk. XIII, Chap. 16, and Bk. XVIII, Chap. 41, Bk. XIX, Chap. 18, and Dooyeweerd, *New Critique*, p. 507.

[31] Dooyeweerd, *loc. cit.*, p. 509.

Dooyeweerd believes that his work ought to be called Christian philosophy without further restrictions, for the essence of a Christian philosophy is its submission to Biblical revelation and its abandonment of the autonomy of reason.[32]

As Dooyeweerd understands the Reformation, it provided the framework in which a Christian philosophy could develop. For it viewed Holy Scripture as the norm of theology and philosophy and thus should have led to an inner reformation of the latter. But the influence of the scholastic motive of nature and grace was too strong to be overcome by Christian philosophy and Luther, in spite of his confession of divine grace, never escaped the influence of Occamism, and he never sought a radical reformation of philosophy itself.[33]

The influence of Melanchton was responsible for the return to the scholastic view of accommodation, and during the next centuries it prevented the development of a reformation philosophy[34] by the establishment of a synthesis between the Lutheran faith and a nominalistically interpreted Aristolelianism.

Calvin's Augustinian recognition that the nature of man has been corrupted by the fall, and is restored by God's grace in Christ, signified a break with scholasticism in philosophy. Knowledge, and especially the knowledge of faith, is rooted for Calvin in the heart, from whence proceeds the issues of life.

Dooyeweerd appeals to Calvin's essentially Augustinian position that reason has been "corrupted that it not only needed to be healed, but nearly to assume a new nature."[35]

Dooyeweerd agrees with Calvin further in the latter's rejection of rationalistic scholasticism:

And it will not have been sufficient that the mind is illuminated by the Spirit of God, unless also by its virtue the heart is made firm and is strengthened. In this matter, the scholastics completely deviate, which in a superficial way conceive the motive of faith as a mere

---

[32] *Ibid.*, p. 525.
[33] *Ibid.*, pp. 511-512.
[34] *Ibid.*, p. 513.
[35] *Ibid.*, p. 516.

and simple assent by virtue of the understanding, whereas the confidence and surety of the heart is completely neglected.[36]

And also with Calvin's rejection of speculative natural theology when Calvin writes:

> Hence we understand that this is the most correct way and appropriate order to seek God; not that in an audacious curiosity we try to penetrate into an examination of his essence, which is rather to be adored than scrupulously to be examined (*Inst.* 1, 5, 9).

This does not mean that Dooyeweerd would seek a philosophical system in Calvin or that he would canonize a philosophical system. But with Calvin, Dooyeweerd rejects every conception of philosophy which affirms the self-sufficiency of reason, and he would relate philosophical thought in its foundation and starting point to the Christian religion.[37]

But in spite of Dooyeweerd's avowed Augustinian view of philosophy, he believes that the significance of his own philosophy is not limited to Christian thought, for he holds that it has raised new problems, opened the way for a better understanding between various conflicting schools, and made a positive contribution by disclosing hitherto uninvestigated states of affairs belonging to the structure of empirical reality.[38]

In setting forth Dooyeweerd's conception of the relationship between philosophy and theology, it will become necessary for us to assess the validity of his claim to universal philosophical significance. For it may be that Dooyeweerd occupies a place within the history of Augustinianism, but that the nature of the latter bars him from philosophical circles which are unwilling to unite religious belief and theoretical activity.

Dooyeweerd is, however, aware of this objection to the traditional Augustinian position and his originality consists in part in his defense of such a synthesis by means of a critical analysis of theoretical thought, to which we shall now turn in detail.

[36] *Idem.*
[37] *Ibid.*, p. 522.
[38] *Ibid.*, pp. 526, 527.

Dooyeweerd's Critique of Reason

In keeping with the Augustinian tradition, Dooyeweerd is, as we have seen, unwilling to separate reason from faith in the divine revelation in Christ.[39] Like Augustine, Dooyeweerd was for a time under the influence of what he considered to be non-Christian philosophy: neo-Kantianism and Husserl's phenomenology.[40] A change took place, however, when Dooyeweerd discovered the religious foundation of reason, and then undertook, on the basis of this discovery to transform philosophy by relating it to Christian revelation.

Dooyeweerd is convinced of the legitimacy of the introduction of theology into philosophy because he believes that human experience and the world of experience are not neutral or capable of being neutral with respect to religion. Thus the Augustinian synthesis between faith and reason is not simply a voluntary choice made by the philosopher, but it is a necessary choice, one which is unavoidable to the non-Christian, as well as to the Christian.[41]

Dooyeweerd's critical justification of a synthesis between philosophy and theology is based on an analysis of the history of philosophy and on an analysis of reason, or what he prefers to call theoretical thought.

Dooyeweerd is aware that his philosophy is complex and complicated because it breaks with much of the philosophical tradition.

He who will make it his own must try to follow step by step its turns of thought, and penetrate behind the theoretical structure to the religious basic attitude of this whole mode of philosophizing. . . . to those who are not ready in reading to free themselves from

[39] Cf. Augustine's *Confessions*, Bk. VI, Chap. 7:8. "Thus much I believed, at one time more strongly than another, yet did I ever believe both that thou wert, and hadst a care of us, although I was ignorant both what was to be thought of thy substance, and what way led, or led back, to thee. Seeing then that we were too weak by unaided reason to find out the truth and for this cause needed the authority of the holy writings."

[40] *New Critique*, Vol. I, p. vi.

[41] *Ibid.*, p. viii.

the traditional views of reality and epistemology and who look at merely isolated subsections of the work, this philosophy will not open its meaning.[42]

And as historians we can agree with Dooyeweerd further that:

Nobody can get rid of this view by ignoring it. As little as Christian thought can isolate itself in an attitude of negation toward non-Christian philosophy, so little may the latter adopt such an attitude toward this trend of Christian philosophy.[43]

To appeal to the authority of a long philosophical tradition is an insufficient reason, in Dooyeweerd's opinion, for the rejection of his religious standpoint. For it is precisely the objective character of this tradition that he would call into question.[44] It begs the question to assume at the outset that Dooyeweerd's philosophy is without scientific interest because it rests upon a religious basis. For he recognizes that the introduction of unnecessary presuppositions into scientific activity is disturbing and damaging to scientific investigation. He is convinced, however, that there are certain presuppositions which are necessary, in that they constitute the very conditions under which philosophical activity can take place.

The problem for Dooyeweerd is how can one distinguish between necessary and unnecessary presuppositions in philosophy, for in answering this very question certain necessary non-theoretical presuppositions are in effect pressupposed with respect to the nature of scientific thought.[45]

It is for Dooyeweerd uncritical to assume that scientific and philosophical activity can exist apart from necessary non-theoretical *a priori* principles. To hold to the autonomy of theoretical thought is for Dooyeweerd itself a presupposition. The very postulate of the inner self-sufficiency of theoretical

[42] *Ibid.*, pp. viii, ix.
[43] *Idem.*
[44] See Herman Dooyeweerd. "De Niet-theoretische voorordelen in de Wetenschap," *Philosophia Reformata*, 3jg. 4e (Kwaartal, Kampen, 1936), pp. 194 ff.
[45] *Ibid.*, p. 193.

thought is a presupposition of a non-theoretical nature, and not to recognize it as such is to be dogmatic. And one of Dooyeweerd's prime concerns is to combat such dogmatism.

The basic thesis that Dooyeweerd seeks to defend throughout his entire writings is that, even in its own domain, philosophical thought is not independent of non-philosophical, religious motives.[46] A religiously neutral objective position is impossible. Modern philosophy erroneously supposed that its assumptions were merely theoretical, and that philosophy is as valid in its methods and doctrines as physics or mathematics. Modern philosophy itself rests upon a religious conviction, a trust in man and in science.[47]

Dooyeweerd's thesis depends partly on his conception of the nature of philosophy and partly on his view of theoretical activity in general. Philosophy is an activity which is inseparable from the philosopher.[48] Its very actuality presupposes an existential relationship between philosophical thinking and the thinking self. This basically personal and subjective view of philosophy shows a certain affinity to certain forms of existentialism, which also denies the autonomy and objectivity of philosophy.[49] But Dooyeweerd's basic Augustinian conviction that the world examined by the philosopher has been created with a God-given structure distinguishes him from the existentialists who allow for no structure in experience that is not the product of human subjectivity.

Dooyeweerd assumes that philosophy examines a created world and that as such the world is dependent upon God. The world has meaning [*Sinn*] only in its subordination to God, and its various aspects or modes are themselves expressions of meaning. Meaning [*Sinn*] is for Dooyeweerd *das Sein des Seienden*, the mode of being of all that is created.

[46] Herman Dooyeweerd, "Het Dilemma voor het Christelijk Wijsgeerig Denken en Het Critisch Karakter van de Wijsbegeerte der Wetsidee," *Philosophia Reformata*, Jg. le (Kwaartal, Kampen, 1936), p. 3.

[47] Richard Kroner, Untitled book review, *Review of Metaphysics*, Vol. VIII, No. 2 (December, 1954).

[48] Dooyeweerd, *New Critique*, p. 5.

[49] For example, cf. Jean Paul Sartre's, *Existentialism is a Humanism* (New York: Philosophical Library, 1947), which assigns priority to human subjectivity.

To ordinary experience, which is primary for Dooyeweerd, the aspects of experience are not distinct and separate. And no matter how many abstract divisions and distinctions science and philosophy may make, temporal reality remains a unity so that the fields investigated by the various sciences are abstract perspectives of the external world.[50]

When philosophy functions properly, it is concerned with the totality of the cosmos.[51] The self, active in philosophy, has many other functions and is in fact a concentration point which cannot be explained in terms of any function or combination of functions. The self, a subjective totality, is the presupposition of all activity, and to acquire knowledge of the self, the limits of philosophical thought must be surpassed. For the self which thinks theoretically cannot itself be the product of an abstraction of thought. The ego transcends thought and it is this thought-transcending ego which is presupposed by philosophical self-reflection.[52]

Philosophy is able to gain a total view of the world of experience only if the philosopher chooses a point of reference outside of experience. Such a fixed point, the product of self-transcendence, goes beyond a theoretical concept, and is attainable in a non-theoretical idea, or limiting concept. The fixed point which permits the formation of an idea of experience in its totality is called by Dooyeweerd "The Archimedean Point" of philosophy.[53]

The problem of the total view of reality, attainable in the self-transcendance of philosophical thought requires a further non-philosophical notion of the *arché* or origin of the diversity and unity of cosmic reality.

Dooyeweerd presupposes that philosophical thought cannot avoid a decision with respect to the origin of the cosmos.[54]

[50] Dooyeweerd, *New Critique*, Vol. I, p. 3.
[51] *Ibid.*, p. 4.
[52] *Ibid.*, pp. 6, 7. Cf. St. Augustine, *City of God*, Bk. XI, Chap. 26, 27. See further, *Concerning Two Souls, Against the Manicheans*, Bk. I, Chap. 3; Bk. I, Chap. 5.
[53] Dooyeweerd, *loc. cit.*, pp. 8 ff.
[54] *Ibid.*, p. 9.

Such a committment with respect to the origin of our knowledge and of knowable reality lies at the foundation of philosophical thought.

The tendency of philosophy to seek the origin of experience is due to the fact that our soul is restless until it finds its beatitude in God.[55]

And from the fact that philosophy requires self-reflection, a view of the *arché* of our selfhood, and a view of the totality of our cosmos, in which the ego participates, Dooyeweerd concludes that the ego itself obeys a law from which it derives its meaning and by which it is limited.[56]

. . . Philosophic thought presupposes an Archimedean point for the thinker, from which our ego in the philosophic activity of thought can direct its view of totality over the modal diversity of meaning. Secondly, it presupposes a choice of position in the Archimedean point in the fact of the arché, which transcends all meaning and in which our ego comes to rest in the process of philosophic thought.[57]

To seek the starting point of philosophy (i.e., what Dooyweerd calls the Archimedean point) in theoretical thought renders it unsuitable as a point of reference from which a total view of reality in its unity and diversity can be gained.

The diversity of cosmic reality is transcended in the center of human existence, so that the starting point of philosophy is connected with the subjective self. But unlike Descartes, Dooyeweerd does not seek the starting point of philosophical thought within philosophical thought. Philosophy which seeks its starting point within the latter is called by Dooyeweerd "immanence philosophy," and the latter includes non-Christian philosophy in all its various manifestations.[58]

Philosophy for Dooyeweerd is in need of a starting point outside of the diversity of experience and one which is not

[55] Cf. St. Augustine, *The Confessions,* Bk. VIII, Chap. 12.
[56] *Ibid.,* p. 11.
[57] *Idem.*
[58] *Ibid.,* p. 14.

equivalent to the unity of cosmic reality. Cosmic diversity (i.e., reality considered in its various aspects) is not identical with distinctions which are the result of logical analysis. For the logical function of thought is itself a part of cosmic diversity, and logical analysis is therefore not the origin of cosmic diversity.[59] To consider cosmic diversity as the product of logical analysis is to detach the logical function from cosmic diversity and to absolutize it as the *arché* of experience. And such an act is religious because it is an assumption with respect to the *origin* of meaning. To proclaim the self-sufficiency of philosophy absolutizes a human function and therefore is not a purely theoretical act, but is prejudiced in a religious sense. "The selfhood as the religious root of existence is the hidden player on the instrument of philosophic thought."[60]

Dooyeweerd assumes that because it is the ego which philosophizes, the ego is the central point of reference and the deeper unity beyond, and above all diversity of experience. And yet there is no aspect of our cosmos in which the ego does not function. And without critical self-reflection a concept of the totality of cosmic experience is unattainable. Self-reflection presupposes that the ego directs itself toward itself and the return to oneself transcends the limits of philosophical thought.

The idea of the totality of experience toward which philosophy strives is empty unless the ego participates in the totality, and to find a vantage point, from which cosmic diversity can be viewed in its unity, we must be able to find a standpoint which transcends a special aspect of experience.

To understand its own meaning, the ego seeks its origin and the origin of all meaning, the origin of our entire cosmos. And the choice of origin is religious, a commitment. For, self-knowledge, and knowledge of the origin, exceeds the limits of theoretical discussion and is rooted in the "heart," the religious center of existence. In consequence, Dooyeweerd concludes that philosophy is by its very nature connected with a

[59] *Ibid.*, pp. 16, 19.
[60] *Ibid.*, p. 21.

religious act. It cannot be neutral, for the very proclamation of its neutrality is a religious choice of origin.

In itself philosophic thought offers no starting point, for it functions only within a cosmic coherence, and the different aspects of experience, which constitute the unity of reality, are not to be transcended at any point by theoretical thought.

The very idea of coherence of cosmic diversity is a limiting concept which discloses that theoretical thought is not self-sufficient. And this inter-modal coherence can be transcended solely in the religious root of existence.

Since the publication of Dooyeweerd's major, three volume work in Dutch, *De Wysbegeerte der Wetsidee*,[61] Dooyeweerd has concentrated on sharpening his criticism. And in the English translation and revision of his work[62] he recognizes that if he is to avoid the charge of dogmatism, and if his critique is to embrace every view of philosophy, it is necessary to broaden his critique to include the "theoretical attitude of thought as such. For no veritable philosophy whatsoever can escape this attitude."[63]

The fact that the autonomy of theoretical thought meant something different to the Greeks than it does to the Thomist and the humanist suggests to Dooyeweerd that it is dogmatic to make it a scientific axiom, and that a critical spirit requires a critical inquiry at the very beginning of philosophical reflection "into the universally valid conditions which alone make theoretical thought possible, and which are required by the immanent structure of this thought itself."[64]

Dooyeweerd approaches the problem of the autonomy of theoretical thought via a series of three basic problems, the first of which seeks to determine what it is that the theoretical attitude abstracts from the structures of empirical reality, as these structures are given in everyday experience. And it seeks

---

[61] (Amsterdam: H. J. Paris, 1936.)
[62] *A New Critique of Theoretical Thought,* in 4 Vols.
[63] *Ibid.,* Vol. I, p. 35.
[64] *Ibid.,* p. 37.

to determine the conditions under which such abstraction is possible.[65]

In dealing with the nature of the given, Dooyeweerd assumes that the data which presents itself for theoretical analysis appears in its truly empirical form in an integral, uninterrupted coherence, a coherence of which we are immediately and intuitively aware. As given, reality is in a state of indissoluble interrelation. A pre-theoretical view of reality discloses an indissoluble inner coherence which binds the

... numerical to the spatial, the latter to the aspect of mathematical movement, the aspect of movement to that of physical energy, which itself is the necessary basis of the aspect of organic life. The aspect of organic life has an inner connection with that of psychical feeling, the latter refers in its logical anticipation (the feeling of logical correctness or incorrectness) to the analytical-logical aspect. This in turn is connected with the historical, the linguistic, the aspect of social intercourse, the economic, the aesthetic, the jural, the moral aspects and that of faith.[66]

What is actually a unity as originally experienced, is contemplated as distinct only in an artificial theoretical attitude. Empirical reality as given is a unified structure. In theoretical thought, however, the given is separated into diverse aspects, and is contemplated in terms of particular modes, in an antithetic structure. Empirical reality is rent asunder by abstraction, and our analytical function opposes the non-logical aspects of experience, thereby constituting the latter as *Gegenstand* to the aspect of analytical distinction.

The antithetic structure of the theoretical attitude occurs within thought, not within the external world. It is intentional, not an ontical structure. That is to say, the antithetical structure of theoretical thought refers exclusively to a mental state of affairs, and does not refer to empirical reality in its integral sense, which includes all modal aspects and individual things.

A serious confrontation of the pre-theoretical attitude with

[65] *Ibid.*, p. 41.
[66] *Ibid.*, p. 3.

the theoretical attitude of thought reveals to Dooyeweerd that the antithetic structure of the theoretical attitude does not correspond to the structure of empirical reality. It is a consequence of theoretical abstraction, and when it is realized that the theoretical attitude arises only in an abstraction, theoretical reason cannot be regarded as an unproblematic datum.[67]

In the theoretical attitude non-logical aspects stand in an intentional antithesis to the logical function. The aspects opposed to the logical (x), is theoretically distinguished from the remaining aspects (y), and (x) is also in an antithetic relation to (y).

The problem of concept formation is connected for Dooyeweerd with this antithetic gegenstand-relation. For any attempt to grasp the non-logical aspects in a logical concept meets wih resistance, because even when theoretically abstracted (x) coheres with (y) which has not been selected as the field of inquiry.

In everyday common sense experience, called by Dooyeweerd "naive experience," our logical function remains interwoven with other aspects or modes of being. And concept formation on this common sense level is not concerned with abstract relations but with concrete events and things, so that the logical structure of thought is joined in an indissoluble coherence with non-logical aspects, and the logical aspect is thus an implicit component of concrete reality.[68]

Within naive experience concrete things are comprehended in the structural relation of subject and object, and the latter relation is thought of as belonging to reality itself, consequently, reality is here experienced in the total and integral coherence of its aspects.[69] The subject-object relation is therefore not to be identified with the gegenstand-relation. The former belongs to the pre-theoretical attitude of experience and leaves reality intact, and the latter constitutes the theoretical attitude and sets reality apart in the diversity of modal aspects.

The problem of the intended antithesis characteristic of the

[67] *Ibid.*, pp. 38-40.
[68] *Ibid.*, p. 42.
[69] *Ibid.*, p. 43.

theoretical attitude raises the further problem of theoretical synthesis, for the theoretical function of thought seeks to overcome the resistance offered by the non-logical *Gegenstand* and to form a logical concept by uniting the logical and non-logical aspects. The second transcendental problem of theoretical thought is therefore:

From what standpoint can we reunite synthetically the logical and the non-logical aspects of experience which were set apart in opposition to each other in the theoretical antithesis?[70]

By raising this question, Dooyeweerd seeks to show that the dogma of the autonomy of theoretical thought is incompatible with the intentional structure of the theoretical attitude, and thereby to subject every starting point of theoretical thought to a basic criticism.[71] For the antithetic relation does not offer a point of synthesis between the logical aspect and its non-logical "Gegenstand." The starting point of theoretical synthesis must, therefore, be sought outside of the antithetic relation. The starting point of theoretical thought necessarily transcends the aspects that have been set apart, or it is unable to relate them to a deeper radical unity.

To seek the starting point of theoretical synthesis within theoretical reason is to absolutize an intentional structure and to fall into dogmatism. For the number of possible modalities of synthesis are equal to the number of non-logical modal aspects. Isms result wherever a specific scientific point of view, whether, for example, mathematical, biological, physical, psychological, or historical, is proclaimed to be the starting point from which a theoretical perspective of empirical reality is to be acquired.[72]

[70] *Ibid.*, p. 45.
[71] Cf. Herman Dooyeweerd, "De transcendentale critiek van het wysgeerig denken en de grondslagen van de wysgeerige denkgemeenschap van het avondland," *Philosophia Reformata*, 6e jg, pp. 1:20.
[72] *Ibid.*, Vol. I, p. 46. Cf. H. Dooyeweerd, "Introduction a une critique transcendentale de la pensée philophique," *Melanges Philosophiques*, Bibliotheque de Xme Congres International de Philosophie (Amsterdam: L. J. Veen, 1952), II, pp. 70-82.

The choice of a theoretical aspect in terms of which a theoretical vision of reality is sought is never theoretically justifiable. Not only does the antithetic structure of thought resist the reduction of one aspect to another, but such absolutizing results in antinomies and does not account for the fact that the theoretical attitude is based upon the antithetic relation, and theoretical synthesis cannot cancel the antithetic relation, for such would be a cancellation of the theoretical attitude. Theoretical synthesis presupposes a supra-theoretical starting point above theoretical diversity, from which theoretical synthesis is performed.

Thus the second transcendental problem leads to a quest for a deeper unity outside of the polar antithesis between the logical and non-logical aspects. As long as our attention is directed toward opposed modal aspects, theoretical thought is unable to discover the sought after starting point.

And the deeper unity above the polar opposites is to be found in critical self-reflection. For

... only when theoretical thought is directed to the thinking ego, does it acquire the concentric direction towards an ultimate unity of consciousness which must lie at the root of all modal diversity of meaning.[73]

... Human I-ness functions, to be sure, in all modal aspects of reality. But it is nevertheless, a central and radical unity, which as such transcends all temporal aspects. The way of critical self-reflection is, consequently, the only one that can lead to the discovery of the true starting point of theoretical thought.[74]

The theoretical perspective of the mutual relations and coherence of the modal aspects presupposes a theoretical vision of reality, a view of the abstracted modal aspects in the totality of their coherence. It presupposes a basic denominator under which the non-logical aspects can be compared. Otherwise the aspect could not be distinguished.[75] The starting point chosen

---

[73] *Ibid.*, Vol. I, p. 51.

[74] *Ibid.*, p. 51.

[75] Cf. Herman Dooyeweerd, *De beteekenis der wetsiden voor Rechts wetenschap en Rechts-philosophie* (Kampen: J. H. Kok, 1926), pp. 14 ff.

for theoretical synthesis is decisive for the vision of the mutual relationship and coherence of the modal aspects.[76] And the search for the starting point of theoretical synthesis again involves a transition from the theoretical to the religious sphere, since questions of self-knowledge are religious questions, and theoretical synthesis presupposes critical self-reflection.[77]

The third transcendental problem with which a critique of theoretical thought is concerned is thus: "How is this critical self-reflection, this concentric direction of theoretical thought to the I-ness, possible, and what is its true character?"[78]

Theoretical thought does not contain a starting point for the inter-modal synthesis. Therefore, the concentric direction of theoretical thought, necessary for self-reflection, does not have a theoretical origin. It springs rather from the ego, the center of human existence. And the selfhood which directs theoretical thought necessarily concentrates upon the origin of all meaning, so that in Augustinian fashion, Dooyeweerd again presupposes that self-knowledge depends upon knowledge of God.[79]

Self-knowledge and the knowledge of the origin are found outside of theoretical thought, in the "heart," the religious center of existence. And yet although self-knowledge is admittedly supra-theoretical it is not irrelevant to theoretical thought. For without self-knowledge the starting point of theoretical synthesis is unknown.

Dooyeweerd is aware that he has made a leap from the theoretical to the religious. It is, however, his contention that such a transition is necessary. The problem for the historian is, however, whether or not the leap from the concentric direction of theoretical thought, to the self as the religious center of consciousness, is a warranted leap. And the further question arises as to what is here understood by religion.

Dooyeweerd does not overlook the problem of whether or

[76] Dooyeweerd, *New Critique*, Vol. 1, p. 48.
[77] *Ibid.*, p. 50.
[78] *Ibid.*, p. 52.
[79] *Ibid.*, pp. 54 ff.

not his criticism moves in a vicious circle. For does proof of any kind not presuppose the very autonomy of theoretical thought, the impossibility of which Dooyeweerd would demonstrate?

Dooyeweerd believes that such an objection is met if it is remembered that what is stringently proven is that self-reflection cannot arise in the theoretical attitude, but can issue only from the ego as a supra-theoretical center. Up until this point his criticism simply discloses structural states of affairs. Dooyeweerd admits, however, that:

> It is, of course, impossible that this transcendental criticism although up to the question of self-knowledge being of a strictly theoretical character—itself should be unprejudiced. For in this case it would refute its own conclusion. But what shall we say, if the very supra-theoretical presuppositions hold here, which free theoretical thought from dogmatic "axioms" standing in the way of veritable critical attitude? If, as we have demonstrated, theoretical synthesis is possible only from a supra-theoretical starting point, then only the contents of the supra-theoretical presuppositions implied thereby, can be questionable, but not the very necessity of them.[80]

Dooyeweerd believes, therefore, that it is possible to demonstrate that the starting point of theoretical thought cannot be found in thought itself, but is supra-theoretical. He does not hold, however, that the religious content of his own starting point can be theoretically demonstrated. That self-knowledge and the knowledge of God is found in the Biblical revelation of God as the absolute origin, is not a scientific fact, but the result of a religious commitment. Dooyeweerd does not seek to prove the existence of God or to prove that God has expressed his image in man by concentrating the entire temporal existence of the cosmos in the radical religious unity of the ego. Such religious dogmas belong to the content of self-knowledge and can never be proven theoretically. Dooyeweerd's contention is only that self-knowledge is necessary, for without it the starting point of theoretical synthesis is unintelligible. That the starting point of theoretical thought is found solely in the

[80] *Ibid.*, p. 56.

central religious sphere of consciousness is an Augustinian, religious affirmation, which Dooyeweerd does not expect other philosophers to admit. The point that he believes he has proven, however, is that the dogma of the autonomy of theoretical thought is not religiously neutral but depends upon a religious view of the self, even if the latter is simply a denial of the self.

By religion in this context, Dooyeweerd simply understands an "innate impulse of the human self-hood to direct itself toward the true or toward a pretended absolute origin of all temporal diversity of meaning, which it finds focused concentrically in itself."[81]

Dooyeweerd believes that religion is the function of relating the various aspects of experience to the self and to an origin. Man is a religious animal. Religion is the most basic element of human nature, and as such religion cannot be defined in terms of any aspect of experience. The inner essence of religion is not simply an emotional feeling, capable of psychological description. But the very "mode of being of the ego itself is of a religious character."[82]

The inner point of contact between philosophic thought and religion is, therefore, evident for Dooyeweerd from the structure of theoretical thought, since theoretical synthesis supposes a religious starting point. For theoretical synthesis requires critical self-reflection and self-knowledge which is religious in character.

The religious starting point of philosophy and of theoretical thought is not purely individual. For man is a part of a spiritual community. A religious *Grundmotif* directs the spirit of a community and forms its attitude and thought.

Dooyeweerd believes with Augustine that since the fall into sin there have been two driving motives behind human activity: the dynamic of the Holy Ghost, which redirects man to God, and the spirit of apostasy from the true God.[83]

[81] *Ibid.*, p. 57.
[82] *Ibid.*, p. 58.
[83] Cf. Augustine, *The City of God.*

Historical investigation discloses for Dooyeweerd that basic religious motives directed the development of philosophy in different ways at different times, but the course of philosophic thought was always directed by a triad of transcendental Ideas corresponding to the three basic problems of theoretical thought.[84]

The transcendental theoretical ideas are concerned with the coherence, totality, and origin of all meaning. It relates the aspects of experience, which have been analytically separated, to the presupposita which made theoretical distinctions possible.[85]

The question of the mutual relation and coherence of modal aspects, the question of their religious root, which expresses their totality of meaning, and the question of origin, constitute three aspects of a single problem, answerable in terms of a transcendental basic idea, the basic idea of all philosophy; and the content of the latter is directly determined by a religious motive.[86]

The basic Idea of philosophy enables us to comprehend the limits of philosophy. It is, therefore, a limiting concept or hypothesis, in which we retire into ourselves. The presupposita of philosophy, to which the basic Idea of philosophy refers, are more than ideas.[87]

Traditional metaphysical speculation and natural theology are rejected by Dooyeweerd on the ground that philosophy is possible only within the temporal order. The religious presupposition of a Christian philosophy is of a transcendent nature, but philosophy itself is confined to the empirical order.[88]

The basic Idea of philosophy is admittedly a subjective—although necessary—hypothesis.[89] It remains bound to the tem-

[84] *Ibid.*, Vol. I, p. 68. Cf. *Reformatie en Scholastick in de Wijsbegeerte*, Vol. I, pp. 30 ff.
[85] *Ibid.*, p. 69.
[86] *Ibid.*, pp. 70 ff.
[87] *Ibid.*, p. 87.
[88] *Ibid.*, p. 88.
[89] *Ibid.*, p. 91.

poral order.[90] And God alone is above the laws and norms of our world. The hypothesis of philosophy, the transcendental basic idea, is an idea of cosmic law, and is therefore referred · to by Dooyeweerd by the term "cosmonomic Idea." And each system of philosophy is directed by such an *a priori* conception of the origin and totality of meaning of the cosmic order. The term "cosmonomic Idea" refers to the order of the cosmos.[91] It points to the factual side of reality.

The central motive of the Christian religion supplies Dooyeweerd's "cosmonomic Idea" with its content. And this Biblical religious motive finds theoretical expression throughout Dooyeweerd's philosophy. The Archimedean point of philosophy is found in Christ, the new religious root of the cosmos. From this root regenerate mankind receives its spiritual life. Thus Dooyeweerd shares Augustine's religious attitude in philosophy, and seeks the origin of law and of individual subjectivity in God's sovereign creative will.

Dooyeweerd's Interpretation of the History of Philosophy

Dooyeweerd distinguishes four religious basic motives in Western thought, the motive of classic antiquity: form and matter; the motive of the Christian religion as expressed by Augustine, and to which Dooyeweerd adheres—creation, the fall, and redemption; a scholastic synthesis between the first two—nature and grace; and, finally, the motive of modern humanism—freedom and nature.

From its inception Dooyeweerd believes that Greek thought was dominated by the motive of *morphé* and *hulé,* which although named by Aristotle, was in fact in control throughout classic antiquity.

This motive of matter and form originated from the contact made by the pre-Homeric religions with the cultural religion of the Olympic Gods.[92] Within the pre-Homeric religions of

[90] *Ibid.,* p. 92.
[91] *Ibid.,* p. 96.
[92] Dooyeweerd, *Reformatie en Scholastiek in De Wijsbegeerte,* pp. 21 ff.

nature, a single motive was especially active: the motive of the divine eternally flowing stream of life, which arises out of mother earth, and out of which proceed periodically the generation of individual things which remain subject to the blind *Anangke*.[93]

The motive of form, however, originated in the more recent Olympian religion of form, measure and harmony, the religion of rational form. But the latter was unsuccessful in its attempt to assimilate the older motive of matter, since it did not deal adequately with the problem of life and death, and because it came into conflict with popular conceptions of morality.[94] In consequence a religious dialectical tension arose in Greek thought. And because of the religious character of the form-matter motive, a veritable synthesis remained impossible.[95]

Primacy was subsequently assigned either to form or to matter, but the two remained antithetic to each other throughout antiquity. The first phase of Greek philosophy assigned primacy to the motive of matter up until Parmenides.[96] What Aristotle later designated by the term *hulé*, and what Hesiod called "chaos," received various names in pre-Socratic philosophy and was deified and proclaimed to be the sole *arché* of everything which appeared in a fixed form. This formless and fluid *arché* is identical with what older Greek thinkers understand by *physis*. By the latter the pre-Socratic understood an animated divine force, a flowing continuum filled with divine life, and eternally in motion.[97]

In Anaximander *physis* becomes the *Apeiron*.[98] In Heraclitus, the motive of matter is joined with the motive of form in the notion of the *logos* which governs the process of eternal flux according to a rational order and harmony. The blind un-

---

[93] *Ibid.*, p. 23.
[94] *Ibid.*, p. 27.
[95] *Ibid.*, p. 50.
[96] *Ibid.*, p. 65.
[97] Cf. Thales' Fragment 22, in Diels-Kranz, *Fragment der Vorsokratike*, cited by Dooyeweerd, *ibid.*, p. 66.
[98] *Ibid.*, p. 68.

predictable *Anangké* of the religious motive of matter is thus dialectically related to the *logos* of the religious motive of form.[99]

In Parmenides, however, the principle of matter lost its primacy, and the opposing conceptions of Parmenides and Heraclitus gave rise to a metaphysics of form which sought to penetrate to the hidden supra-sensible essential form of reality which lurks behind the visible phenomena which are subject to the principle of matter.[100]

Thus the primal dualism in the religious basic motive of the Greek community expressed itself in the metaphysical opposition between being and becoming.

The visible world is devoid of all true being. And only *theoria* leads to knowledge of divine *physis* because *theoria* is identical with being.[101]

The Greek concept of *theoria* is thus consciously opposed to the mythological conceptions of popular religion and to common sense. It alone can lead to absolute truth. The Greek conception of the autonomy of reason is, however, radically different from the concept of reason in Thomism or modern humanism. For the *theoria* of the Greeks was rooted in the basic religious motive of Greek thought.[102]

In Plato and Aristotle the principle of matter lost all divine properties but was not eliminated.[103] According to the Aristotelian point of view, every natural substance strives toward its own perfection, enclosed in its essential form. The substantial forms are hierarchically arranged so that the lower is the matter of a higher form. The deity, as pure actual form, is the origin of motion, but not of the principle of matter. Consequently as "actus purus," the *arché* is the final formal ground of being, and "pure matter" is the principle of becoming. There is, however,

[99] *Ibid.,* pp. 69, 70.

[100] *Ibid.,* p. 79.

[101] It is thus that Dooyeweerd interprets Parmenides' statement "Being and thought are identical." *Ibid.,* p. 80.

[102] *Ibid.,* p. 81.

[103] Herman Dooyeweerd, "De Vier Religieus Grondmotifs van het Wijsgeerig Denken van het Avondland," *Philosophia Reformata,* Ge jg (Kwaartal, 1942), pp. 167 ff.

no deeper unity above form and matter.[104] Matter is deprived of divine quality by becoming the principle of imperfection and potentiality.

The second religious motive of creation, the fall and redemption has already been noted. During the Aristotelian Renaissance, the Augustinian-Platonic school was superseded by a conscious attempt to bring about a religious synthesis between a Greek view of nature and the Christian faith.

The autonomy of reason was posited in the sphere of natural knowledge, and nature was considered to be the substructure of super-natural grace.

The inner opposition of the motive of nature and grace ended in the Occamist notion that there is no point of contact between nature and grace.[105]

The collapse of the ecclesiastically unified culture enabled the nominalism of the 14th century to pave the way for humanism by destroying the Thomist synthesis. The Christian and pagan motives were radically disrupted, nature and grace were completely separated and humanism was free to develop the notion of "autonomous natural reason."[106]

Modern humanism developed the basic religious motive of nature and freedom by secularizing the Biblical motive of creation and freedom.[107] The latter is expressed in a religion of human personality; it produces a desire to dominate nature, and thus leads to a religion of autonomous objective science, which excludes a free personality. The motive of freedom in humanism rejected all faith in authority and demands the absolute autonomy of human personality. In seeking to satisfy the latter demand, humanism viewed nature as an object that could be dominated by an autonomous science. It sought to comprehend the phenomena of nature in a system of functional

[104] Herman Dooyeweerd. "De idee der individualiteitis-structuur en het Thomistische substantiebegrip, *Philosophia Reformata*, 8e, j8, 3e (Kwaartal, 1944), Vol. 8, 9, 10.

[105] Dooyeweerd, *New Critique*, Vol. 1, p. 186.

[106] *Ibid.*, pp. 183, 188.

[107] *Ibid.*, pp. 190 ff.

causal relations, in terms of their mathematical and physical aspects.[108] By construing reality in terms of the new scientific method, the cosmos became the construction of mathematical natural science, and all phenomena of nature were ordered in a continuous causal series which did not permit the freedom of human personality. As long as the religious motive of the domination of nature did not lead to a deterministic view of nature, the conflict with the motive of freedom was not brought to the surface.[109]

Descartes' reconstruction of the data of experience via a methodological scepticism illustrates the religious motive of the ideal of personality at work. For the sovereign human personality rejected all order which it does not itself prescribe.[110] Sovereign reason thus became the origin of the theoretically construed cosmos and the sovereignty of mathematical thought simply found its support and deification in a secularized notion of God.[111]

Modern philosophy is to be understood in terms of the continual conflict between the free self-sufficient personality and the ideal of science.[112]

The first phase of this conflict is expressed in the conflict between Descartes and Hobbes. Descartes' dualism between "extended body" and "thinking soul" is an arbitrary attempt to save the human personality from being reduced to an object of natural science.[113]

Hobbes, however, would not limit the continuity of the natural science ideal and subsumed all of reality under one metaphysical basic denominator: "the moving body."[114] The recognition of mathematical thought as the *arché* of the diversity of cosmic reality continued, but before primacy was shifted to the ideal of personality, the ideal of science began to free it-

[108] *Ibid.*, p. 193.
[109] *Ibid.*, p. 194.
[110] *Ibid.*, p. 196.
[111] *Ibid.*, p. 197.
[112] *Ibid.*, p. 215.
[113] *Ibid.*, p. 218.
[114] *Ibid.*, p. 217.

self from rationalistic metaphysics, and to seek the common denominator for the different aspects of reality in the psychical function of feeling and sensation.[115] In empiricism the ideal of science took a psychological turn. For the empirical world presented itself solely in psychical impressions and perceptions.[116]

To Locke experience was exhausted by sensation, directed toward the outer world, and reflection, the inner world of the subjective operations of the mind. And the inner perception of the operation of the mind is not possible unless the mind has been stimulated by sensation, so that the understanding owes its content to the psychical ideas given in sensation and reflection.[117]

By dissolving the entire content of knowledge into psychical impressions, the ideal of free creative thought of mathematical science was abandoned in principle, and the science ideal was emancipated from a metaphysics which proclaimed mathematical thought to be the *arché* of the cosmos.[118] And mathematical thought was replaced by psychological thought, which became the basic denominator of cosmic diversity.[119] This shift of the creative function of thought from the mathematical to the psychological reached its climax in Hume, whose system no longer could tolerate the mathematical science-ideal.[120] Moreover, in Hume the psychological ideal of science also destroyed the metaphysical foundation of the ideal of personality by denying the identity of the self-hood:

From thence it evidently follows that identity is nothing really belonging to those different perceptions, and uniting them together; but is merely a quality, which we attribute to them because of the union of their ideas in the imagination, when we reflect upon them.[121]

---

[115] *Ibid.*, pp. 262 ff.
[116] *Ibid.*, p. 263.
[117] *Ibid.*, pp. 264 ff.
[118] *Ibid.*, pp. 271, 277.
[119] *Ibid.*, p. 280.
[120] *Ibid.*, p. 289.
[121] David Hume, *Treatise on Human Nature*, ed. T. H. Green and T. H. Grose (London: Longmans, Green & Co., 1898), Part IV, Sec. VI, p. 540, quoted in Dooyeweerd, *New Critique*, Vol. I, p. 296.

Hume's attack on the foundation of the ideal of personality and on the science-ideal's claim to conceive "nature" in the sense of an outer world, resulted in a tension between the ideal of science and that of personality, a tension which Dooyeweerd regards as a religious crisis, reflected, for example, in Rousseau's recognition of human personality as a moral aim in itself.[122]

Thus in Rousseau, the ideal of personality acquired supremacy over the ideal of science,[123] but the shift in primacy inaugurated a new phase in Kant, a phase in which the ideal of personality liberated itself from the science ideal and restricted the latter to the world of sense-phenomena.[124]

Kant became aware that the sovereign freedom of human personality could not be grasped in the categories of mathematical natural scientific thought.[125] Consequently, he doubted the sovereignty of the latter with respect to the most profound questions of life and the world, and therefore abandoned the metaphysics of the mathematical science ideal to the extent that it disturbed the ideal of personality.[126] Ethics and religion could not be conceived of in the forms of the experience of nature, and metaphysics itself must be barred from the domain of science.[127] Thus Dooyeweerd believes that the rise of Kant's transition to critical idealism was religious, not theoretical.[128] And Kant's removal of the *Ding an sich* from the control of the mathematical ideal of science, his restriction of knowledge to sense phenomena, is also intelligible solely as a religious shift to the motive of freedom, a shift which opened the way to an *a priori* faith in "the reality of the idea of autonomous freedom of human personality."[129]

Thus Dooyeweerd holds that:

[122] *Ibid.*, pp. 313, 314.
[123] *Ibid.*, p. 319.
[124] *Ibid.*, p. 325.
[125] *Ibid.*, p. 331.
[126] *Ibid.*, p. 332.
[127] *Ibid.*, p. 345.
[128] *Ibid.*, p. 351.
[129] *Ibid.*, pp. 354 ff.

The *Critique of Pure Reason* and its counterpart the *Critique of Practical Reason* break the cosmos asunder into two spheres, that of sensory appearance and that of super-sensory freedom,

and that "Kant's Idea of deity as the postulate of 'pure practical reason' is the final hypostatization of the ideal of personality."[130]

Kant's dualistic separation of the realm of nature and freedom is expressed by the statement:

The realm of the nature concept . . . subjected to the laws of the one legislator, and that of the freedom-Idea subjected to those of the other, are completely isolated from each other, precluding all reciprocal influence which they (each according to their basic laws) might have on one another.[131]

It led to the development of a dialectical logic in which nature and freedom could be synthesized in a dialectical way.[132]

Dooyeweerd thus believes that post-Kantian philosophy also in part is an attempt to bridge the religious antithesis in the starting point of humanistic philosophy,[133] an attempt which in Fichte leads to the proclamation of the sovereignty of practical reason in the principle: *"Das Ich setzt sich selbst"* (The ego posits itself).[134] And with Hegel the ideal of personality created its own logic,[135] but Hegel's logicizing of the historical process as a dialectical unfolding, of the absolute spirit in the objective spirit, implied a return to rationalistic view of history, which bound empirical investigation to an *a priori* schematicism.[136]

In the latter half of the 19th century, however, the spiritual uprooting of the religious basic motive of humanism made its appearance in Nietzsche's religion of power which broke with the original religious meaning of nature and freedom, and in which the ideal of science and personality were rejected, thereby

---

130 *Ibid.*, p. 384.
131 *Ibid.*, p. 386.
132 *Ibid.*, p. 402.
133 *Ibid.*, p. 404.
134 *Ibid.*, p. 415.
135 *Ibid.*, p. 472.
136 *Ibid.*, p. 209.

introducing a process of religious decay into Western thought.[137]

Dooyeweerd considers his return to the Augustinian position in philosophy to be a part of a transitional period in which the autonomy of theoretical thought can no longer be held as a philosophic axiom. Anti-humanistic movements, national socialism, fascism, and communism have arisen out of the degeneration of the religious motive of humanism, and his own philosophy is thought to signify a re-awakening of older cultural forces, and to reflect a crisis in the spiritual foundation of Western culture.[138]

[137] *Ibid.,* pp. 211, 212.
[138] *Ibid.,* p. 215.

III. The Neo-Existentialism of Paul Tillich

The Nature of Philosophy and Theology

Tillich formulates the relation between philosophy and theology in terms of theology. Philosophical theology does not deal philosophically with religion as with any other subject, but it is based upon an intrinsic relation between philosophy and theology.[1] Such a confrontation between philosophy and theology is not possible, if philosophy is restricted to logical analysis and epistemological investigation. Consequently, Tillich considers the ontological question as prior to all others and defines philosophy as a cognitive endeavor in which the question of being is asked.[2]

The question of being is the question of what it means to be, of what it means to say that something is. The question of being is not the question of any special being but it is nevertheless an unavoidable question. And Tillich believes that every philosophy has a partial answer to it, whether acknowledged or not, so that ontology is the very core of philosophy.[3] By looking at

[1] Paul Tillich, *The Protestant Era* (Chicago: University of Chicago Press, 1948), p. 83.
[2] Paul Tillich, *Biblical Religion and the Search for Ultimate Reality* (Chicago: University of Chicago Press, 1955), p. 5.
[3] *Ibid.*, p. 6.

things as they are given, it is possible to discover the principles, structure, and the nature of being.[4]

For Tillich, philosophy is thus concerned with being itself; it is an interpretation of being, and not simply an analysis of the sciences, and an attempt to unify their results. Epistemology cannot exist without an ontological basis. For it is impossible to have an appearance without a being that appears, or knowledge apart from a being that is known, or experience without a being that is experienced.[5]

For Tillich, philosophy is a "cognitive approach to reality in which reality as such is the object."[6] Philosophy is concerned with the structures which make experience possible; it examines the structure which makes reality a whole, a potential object of knowledge. To investigate the nature of reality is to inquire into the structures, categories, and concepts presupposed in the cognitive encounter with every realm of reality.[7] Every analysis of the act of knowing refers to an interpretation of being, for knowing is an act which participates in an "ontic relation." The attempt to restrict philosophy to the logic of the sciences need not be taken seriously, if such a restriction is merely a matter of taste. But if such restriction rests on an analysis of the limits of knowledge, an ontological decision concerning the relation between the nature of symbols, signs, and logical operations to reality has to be made, and such implies an answer to the question of the structure of being.[8]

Tillich's theological system incorporates philosophy into the structure of theology by giving theological answers to philosophical questions.[9]

By applying a method of correlation, philosophical analysis of the human situation gives rise to existential questions, and

---

[4] *Ibid.*, p. 8.
[5] Tillich, *The Protestant Era*, p. 86.
[6] Paul Tillich, *Systematic Theology*, Vol. I (Chicago: University of Chicago Press, 1951), p. 18.
[7] *Ibid.*, p. 19.
[8] *Ibid.*, p. 20.
[9] *Ibid.*, p. 30.

theology demonstrates that Christian symbols supply the answer.[10]

Theology is not an empirical-inductive or a metaphysical deductive science. It is based on a personal commitment, and it implies an *a priori* experience and valuation. And yet theology is considered to be a scientific approach to reality in that it employs a method adequate to its subject matter, and thereby discloses "the existential and transcending character of the ground of objects in time and space."

The Christian theologian works with a "mystical *a priori*" and the criterion of the Christian message. He works with the immediate intuitive experience of something ultimate in value,[11] with what is of ultimate concern to him. Theological propositions deal with what can be of ultimate concern for us, i.e., that which determines our being or nonbeing. "Being" here designates the whole of human reality, the structure and meaning of existence.[12] Thus whereas philosophy deals with the structure of being in itself, theology deals with the meaning that being has for us. Theology is existential; it is not detached from its object, since the theologian is determined by his faith.[13]

The experience through which theology becomes aware of its ultimate concern is not the scientific experience of detached observation. The only verification open to the theologian is that of active mystical participation which is beyond experimental verification.[14] Such experience is an inexhaustible source of theological truth, in that the theologian participates directly in religious reality.[15]

The norm of Christian theology is found in the encounter of the Christian church with the Biblical message in the new being as Jesus the Christ, but the meaning of this norm can be understood only with the further development of Tillich's system.[16]

[10] *Ibid.*, p. 62.
[11] *Ibid.*, p. 10.
[12] *Ibid.*, pp. 12 ff.
[13] *Ibid.*, p. 23.
[14] *Ibid.*, p. 44.
[15] *Ibid.*, p. 45.
[16] *Ibid.*, pp. 50 ff.

Because of its mystical intuitive foundation, Tillich's theology does not have a rational character. The object of ultimate concern is not known by rational arguments, but reason is itself supposedly grasped by ultimate concern and by faith. Nevertheless, Tillich would avoid conceptual ambiguity and adhere to the principles of formal logic, so that theology does not utilize a senseless combination of words involving genuine logical contradictions.[17] And yet paradox has a logical place in religion and theology in that God's acting supersedes finite reason but does not annihilate it.

Tillich's View of Reason and Revelation

The view of philosophy which Tillich entertains presupposes that "reason" can be understood in an ontological and a technical sense. Ontological reason is the structure of the mind which makes it possible for the mind to grasp and transform reality, whereas a technical concept of reason reduces reason to "reasoning."

Ontological reason contains a cognitive, aesthetic, practical, and technical function. Reason has a technical aspect, but the latter is not properly detached from its ontological status, a status which permits it to make assertions about the nature of things. Technical reason deals with the discovery of the means of attaining certain ends, but ontological reason provides the ends, since it can grasp reality as it is.[18] Consequently technical reason is itself an expression of ontological reason.

Reason is assumed to be the structure of the mind and reality, a structure which is actual to the extent that its shares in the characteristics of reality and participates in the processes of being, existence, and life.

The concept of ontological reason is thus central to Tillich's system, for he assumes that the mind is able to grasp and shape reality, because, among other things, reality has a logos character.

Tillich distinguishes the rational structure of the mind, sub-

[17] *Ibid.*, p. 56.
[18] *Ibid.*, pp. 72 ff.

jective reason, from the rational-structure of reality, objective reason. The mind is supposedly so constituted that it grasps and shapes reality on the basis of a corresponding structure in reality. Subjective reason is actualized within an individual self. In receiving the mind grasps what is; it penetrates into the essential nature of what is. In reacting the mind shapes what is; it transforms a given material into a structure, a structure with the "power of being."[19]

Reason, conceived of as the universal logos of being, raises the question of revelation by pointing to something beyond itself, to a hidden depth or "ground," a depth which expresses itself in the cognitive realm by pointing to truth itself, to the infinite power of being, the ultimately real. And although this depth of reason is concealed under the conditions of existence, it symbolically discloses itself, in myth and cult.[20]

Reason is driven to seek revelation because of its finitude, its inability to grasp its own infinite ground, and because its own structural elements are in opposition to each other.

The essential unity of reason is broken under the conditions of existence. There is a conflict in reason between "autonomous reason" and "heteronomous reason." Autonomous reason is subject to its own essential structure, implied in the structure of mind and reality, and it refuses to recognize its own depth, whereas heteronomous reason represents the depth of reason, and imposes a strange law upon the structure of reason, in the name of the ground of being. The polar opposition between autonomy and heteronomy produces the quest for theonomy, i.e., reason united with its own depth, so that the quest for revelation arises out of reason itself. For it is God who is the law of the structure and ground of reason, and the attempt to unite the elements of reason is, therefore, a search for God, the quest for revelation.[21]

A second polar opposition within reason itself, that between

[19] *Ibid.*, p. 76.
[20] *Ibid.*, pp. 79, 81.
[21] *Ibid.*, pp. 83, 85.

its static and dynamic elements, leads to the conflict between absolutism and relativism, a conflict that can be overcome solely by the revelation of that which is absolute and concrete at the same time. Reason's static element preserves its identity within the life process, while its dynamic element enables reason to actualize itself within the life process. The static element of reason appears in the absolutism of tradition and of revolution, and its dynamic element in positivistic and cynical relativism.[22]

A third polarity within reason of formal and emotional elements produces the conflict between formalism and irrationalism, out of which the quest for the reconciliation of form and mystery arises.

The conflict within actual reason is allegedly discovered by philosophy, but it is resolved by revelation; and the correlation between philosophy and theology, the possibility of philosophical theology, is assured by the fact that reason is driven to revelation.

For revelation resolves the conflicts of reason by overcoming the conflicts of reason in existence. It reestablishes the essential unity between autonomy and heteronomy by creating a theonomous situation via a final revelation which is completely transparent to the ground of being, and thereby keeps reason from losing its depth. Final revelation, conceived of as the self-sacrifice of the finite medium to the content of revelation, prevents heteronomous reason from establishing itself against rational autonomy in such a way that authority is exercised by a finite being, in the name of the infinite.[23]

Final revelation is symbolized in Jesus as the Christ, in the symbol, "Son of God." For Jesus as the Christ symbolizes an uninterrupted unity with the ground of Jesus' being, and the continuous sacrifice of himself as Jesus to himself as the Christ.[24]

Revelation is thus the manifestation of something inaccessible to the usual means of knowing. It is connected with something

[22] *Ibid.,* pp. 86, 89.
[23] *Ibid.,* pp. 147, 148.
[24] *Ibid.,* pp. 125, 137.

which precedes the subject-object relationship, a dimension of mystery. The essentially mysterious appears within ordinary experience but mystery is not resolved by revelation into knowing. Mystery remains mysterious.[25]

The negative side of mystery "appears when reason is driven beyond itself to its 'ground and abyss,' to that which precedes reason, to the fact that 'being is and non-being is not,' to the original fact that there is something and not nothing."[26]

The positive side of mystery is manifest in actual revelation. And here mystery appears not only as abyss, but as the power of being conquering non-being. It appears as our ultimate concern which is expressed in symbols and myths that point to the depth of reason and to its mystery.

Revelation is, therefore, the manifestation of what concerns us ultimately. And since what is revealed is the ground of our being, it is of ultimate concern to us. Consequently, revelation is invariably for someone in a concrete situation of concern. And there is no revelation apart from someone who receives it as his ultimate concern.

When the mind is grasped by the threat of non-being, the abysmal element, the negative side of the mystery of being, is experienced. Reason experiences an ontological shock; in ecstasy the mind goes beyond itself, beyond its subject-object structure.[27] "Reason reaches its boundary line, is thrown back upon itself, and then is driven again to its extreme situation. . . ." "In revelation and in the ecstatic experience in which it is received the ontological shock is preserved and overcome. . . ."[28]

The experience of the abyss is united in ecstasy with the ground in which reason is grasped by the mystery of its own depth. The cognitive side of ecstasy is inspiration which opens a new dimension of understanding to our ultimate concern, and to the mystery of being.

Tillich does not believe that his conception of revelation can

[25] *Ibid.*, pp. 108 ff.
[26] *Ibid.*, p. 110.
[27] *Ibid.*, p. 112.
[28] *Ibid.*, p. 113.

conflict with reason as the latter is expressed in science, because revelation occurs on a different level. The critical question is, however, not whether Tillich's position is beyond the attacks of science, but whether it refers to any dimension of reality other than that of psychological experience, which would then of course make it vulnerable to psychological investigation.

However, Tillich is unwilling to admit that the notions of "depth of reason," "ground of being," "being itself," rests upon an appeal to psychological states. For he is of the opinion that since every person and thing participates in being-itself, in the ground and meaning of being, every thing or person is a possible bearer of the mystery of being, and can thus become a revelatory medium, by pointing beyond themselves to something which infinitely transcends themselves "to the self-manifestation of that which concerns us ultimately."[29]

For Tillich, language can also be a medium of revelation. For the "word," when it is a medium of revelation, becomes "the Word of God." Such expressions as "Word of God" and "Logos" are symbols. Symbols and signs are not identical although both point beyond themselves to something else.[30] Signs, differ from symbols, however, in that "signs do not participate in the reality and power of that to which they point. Symbols, although they are not the same as that which they symbolize, participate in its meaning and power."[31]

The words of a language become symbols when they acquire connotations which go beyond that to which they point as signs.

"The symbol represents something which is not itself, for which it stands and in the power and meaning of which it participates."[32] It has the function of opening up "levels of reality" otherwise incomprehensible. A symbol opens up levels of reality and it opens up the soul, our interior reality.[33] Unlike signs,

---

[29] *Ibid.,* p. 118.
[30] Paul Tillich, "Religious Symbols and Our Knowledge of God." *The Christian Scholar,* Vol. XXXVII, No. 3 (September, 1955), p. 189.
[31] *Ibid.,* p. 190.
[32] *Idem.*
[33] *Ibid.,* p. 191.

symbols have a special function and cannot be replaced at will by another symbol. Signs are invented, symbols are born out of the "group unconscious" when a group acknowledges its own being in a word or thing.[34]

Religious symbols open up a hidden level of reality, the depth dimension of reality itself, the ground of every other dimension, the level below all other levels, the level of being itself, or the ultimate power of being, the holy.

Religious symbols are born out of a relationship to the ultimate ground of being, ie., to the holy, and they live as long as they continue to open up the experience of depth in the human soul. As symbols of the holy, the ground of being, religious symbols participate in the ground of being, and point symbolically to what transcends them,[35] but, when symbols are identified with the ultimate ground of being, they become demonic.

On the transcendent level, beyond empirical reality, God is the basic symbol.

. . . In our relationship to this ultimate we symbolize and must symbolize. . . . We encounter him with the highest of what we ourselves are, *person*. And so in the symbolic form of speaking about him, we have both that which transcends infinitely our experience of ourselves as persons, and that which is so adequate to our being persons that we can say "Thou" to God, and can pray to him. . . . the qualities, the attributes of God, whatever you say about him: that he is love, . . . mercy, . . . power omniscient, . . . omnipresent . . . are taken from experienced qualities we have ourselves. They cannot be applied to God in the literal sense. If this is done, it leads to an infinite amount of absurdities. . . . the symbolic character of these qualities must be maintained consistently. Otherwise, every speaking about the divine becomes absurd.

We also speak symbolically of "the acts of God." For instance, when we say, "He has created the world," "He has sent his son . . ."

[34] *Ibid.*, p. 192.
[35] *Ibid.*, p. 193.

In all these temporal, causal, and other expressions we speak symbolically of God.[36]

. . . Symbols are independent of any empirical criticism. . . . Their truth is their adequacy to the religious situation in which they are created, and their inadequacy to another situation is their untruth.[37]

Revelation through words are not "revealed words," and as a medium of revelation the word points beyond its denotative and expressive quality to the unexpressible and its relation to us. As a medium of revelation, language is transparent; it discloses the divine mystery and is the "Word of God."

Revelatory power is absent in propositions which give theoretical information about the past,[38] so that any nonexistential concept of revelation is to be rejected.

The "knowledge of revelation" has a special character.

. . . Revealed knowledge lies in a dimension where it can neither be confirmed nor negated by historiography. . . . Knowledge of revelation, although it is mediated primarily through historical events, does not imply factual assertions, and it is therefore not exposed to critical analysis by historical research. Its truth is to be judged by criteria which lie within the dimension of revelatory knowledge.[39]

The Christian claim is that Jesus as the Christ is the decisive revelation. And Tillich seeks to discover criteria that warrant their claim to finality, but not in a literal or traditional sense. The picture of Jesus as the Christ portrays a person who is the medium of final revelation; a person united to the ground of his being, and completely transparent to the mystery he reveals. To be final, a revelation must be able to negate itself without losing itself, and Jesus is the "Son of God," because he met this criterion.

Jesus is the New Creature only in so far as his historical ex-

[36] *Ibid.*, p. 194.
[37] *Ibid.*, p. 196.
[38] Tillich, *Systematic Theology*, p. 123.
[39] *Ibid.*, p. 130.

istence is negated. He is "New Being" to the degree that he is not the old, not finite, not historical. By refusing to be equal with God, he became the Christ.

Jesus is the religious and theological object as the Christ and only as the Christ. And he is the Christ as the one Who sacrifices what is merely "Jesus" in him. The decisive trait in his picture is the continuous self-surrender of Jesus who is Jesus to Jesus who is the Christ.[40]

Christianity is itself not final but it witnesses to the final revelation, to what is final and universal by sacrificing Jesus of Nazareth to Jesus as the Christ.[41]

Such a conception of final revelation is employed by Tillich to unify the conflicts of reason. For, in addition to overcoming the conflict between autonomy and heteronomy, by providing the basis for a new theonomy, final revelation emancipates reason from the conflict between absolutism and relativism by appearing in the form of a concrete absolute. The concrete personal life of Jesus as the Christ unites the conflicting poles of reason, for this New Being is the most concrete of all forms of concreteness, and is the bearer of what is unconditionally absolute.[42]

Final revelation unites the conflict between formalism and emotionalism. For the whole of a person's life participates in the mystery of being, which appears in revelatory experience.[43]

To conceive of revelation as the manifestation of the ground of being for human knowledge assumes that reason has cognitive characteristics relevant to the cognitive character of revelation. The ontological structure of reason is known, and since we have knowledge of its polar structure, we are able to discover existential conflicts which cause reason to seek revelation.[44]

But what does Tillich understand by the term "knowledge" when he claims that we have "knowledge" both of the ontologi-

---

[40] *Ibid.*, p. 134.
[41] *Ibid.*, p. 135.
[42] *Ibid.*, pp. 150, 153.
[43] Ibid., pp. 153, 155.
[44] *Ibid.*, p. 94.

cal structure of reason, and that revelation also yields "knowledge?" The term "knowledge" for Tillich refers to a union between the knower and that which is known, a union in which the gap between subject and object is bridged. "The subject 'grasps' the object, adapts it to itself, and, at the same time, adapts itself to the object." Knowing is thus a form of union, and yet such a union presupposes detachment as its condition; it is a union through separation. To know one must look at a thing and to look at a thing one must be at a distance. "Knowledge" thus refers to a unity of separation and union.

Confirmation of this interpretation of knowledge is found by Tillich in certain aspects of personal and social life; that is to say, it is confirmed existentially under the conditions of existence. The passion to know for the sake of knowing indicates that successful cognition fills a want, a vacuum. Something strange becomes a part of us, and we are driven toward reunion with that to which we belong and which belongs to us. Thus the act of knowledge conquers want and estrangement.

And knowledge also transforms and heals. Since knowledge includes union, it is open to receive that with which it unites. And this is what explains Socrates' assertion that knowing of the good necessitates the doing of the good. The healing and transforming character of knowledge is further confirmed by depth psychology and psychotherapy via psychoanalysis. A further existential confirmation of Tillich's interpretation of knowledge, as a unity between distance and union, is allegedly found in the value assigned to knowledge by integrated human groups.[45]

Every act of knowledge contains an element of union and of detachment, although in different degrees. In "controlling knowledge," the element of detachment plays the major role, and subject and object are united for the sake of the control of the object by the subject, and the object is transformed into a conditioned and calculable "thing." The objectification of controlling knowledge is not only a logical relation but it is also

[45] *Ibid.*, pp. 94, 97.

ontological. In knowing man, however, the element of detachment is secondary and union is primary. Such a cognitive attitude is called "receiving knowledge," knowledge in which the object is united with the subject. In receiving knowledge an emotional element of participation is included, as the vehicle of cognition, but the content of receiving knowledge is rational and capable of verification.

To escape the power of controlling knowledge and the objectified world produced by it, one must again turn to revelation, for the latter creates a complete union with that which appears in revelation, and also satisfies the requirements of detachment and analysis, thereby overcoming the conflict between controlling and receiving knowledge, a conflict rooted in the polar structure of cognitive reason.[46]

Tillich's view of the cognitive nature of philosophy and revelation presupposes a special ontological conception of truth. What does the term "true" mean for Tillich when applied to statements of theology? Obviously "truth" as used by Tillich is not restricted to empirically verifiable statements. The nature of cognitive reason makes it possible to use the predicate "true" for more than analytic sentences or experimentally confirmed propositions.

Judgments for Tillich are true or false to the extent that they grasp or fail to grasp reality. A true judgment states something about reality itself. The true being of things lies hidden under the surface of sense impressions and the seemingly real. And a dialectical approach is needed to penetrate beneath the surface to the really real, the essence of things, their depth, from which they derive their power of being. Appearance is pierced through a process of preliminary affirmations, consequent negations, and final affirmations. The "really real" is grasped, by the mind, and is thus called "true."

Truth, therefore, is the essence of things as well as the cognitive act in which their essence is grasped. The term "truth" is like the term "reason," subjective-objective. A judgment is true because it grasps

[46] *Ibid.*, pp. 97-100.

and expresses true being, and the really real becomes truth if it is grasped and expressed in a true judgment.[47]

The problem immediately arises, however, as to how it is possible to decide the truth or falsehood of a judgment when "truth" applies to the really real. What method could possibly be employed to determine which judgments express true being and which judgments do not?

Tillich is here faced with the problem of showing how truth can be verified outside of the realm of empirical science. For if statements are to be more than tautologies, emotional self-expressions, or meaningless propositions, they must have some means of verification.

Tillich recognizes the principle that "statements which have neither intrinsic evidence nor way of being verified have no cognitive value." But if the verifying test belongs to the nature of truth, how can judgments about the "really real" escape being mere expressions of the subjective state of a person?

The way out of this difficulty is met by Tillich by introducing a method of verification which corresponds for Tillich to receiving knowledge. Tillich assumes that verification can occur within life processes, on an experiential rather than on an experimental level. Experimental verification is thus rejected as the exclusive pattern of all verification. For while experimental verification enjoys the advantage of methodological strictness and the possibility of testing an assertion at every moment, it is, nevertheless, forced to disrupt the totality of life processes, and is not as true to life as is verification of the experiential type.

Controlling knowledge is verified by experiment; "receiving knowledge is verified by the creative union of two natures, that of knowing and that of the known."[48] Such a test is supposedly made by the life process itself, and it is admittedly non-repeatable, lacking in precision, and never final. It is always indefinite and of a preliminary nature, a matter of risk. Future life processes may contradict previous conclusions, and yet experi-

[47] *Ibid.*, p. 102.
[48] *Ibid.*, p. 103.

ential verification must be utilized as the sole test of the truth claim of judgments applicable to the really real!

Because life processes are total in character, spontaneous, and individual, they impose limitations to experiments, since the latter presuppose isolation, regularity, and generality. Life processes can be known only in a creative union. Knowledge of them is verified by participation in them; it is knowledge by participation, by intuition; "the cognitive approach to every individual life process is intuitive."

Thus, the verification of the principles of ontological reason does not rest for Tillich on rational self-evidence or on any pragmatic test, but upon their efficacy in life processes. And the fact that such verification cannot give certainty again leads philosophy to revelation, for the truth of the latter is both ultimately significant and secure.[49]

Being and God

The relationship between reason and revelation is for Tillich secondary to that of the problem of being. Since God is the basic question of theology, and being the basic question of philosophy, an examination of the intrinsic connection between being and God results in a philosophical-theology. For even as an analysis of reason led at every point to the quest for revelation, so an analysis of being serves to introduce the question of God.

Tillich denies that the existence and nature of God is demonstrable by reason. For the concept of existence and the arguments advanced traditionally in support of it, are inadequate to the idea of God, conceived of as the creative ground of essence and existence. To argue that God exists is to deny God, for he is being-itself beyond essence and existence. And to derive God from the world, contradicts the idea of God as that which infinitely transcends the world.

The so-called arguments for the existence of God simply express the question of God, implied in human finitude, as possible and necessary. An awareness of God is present in the ques-

---

[49] *Ibid.*, pp. 100, 105.

tion of God; an awareness of the infinite is contained in man's awareness of finitude. Consequently, in so far as the ontological argument simply describes and analyzes the way in which potential infinity is present in actual infinity, it is valid. For experience provides a practical and theoretical confirmation of the presence of the unconditional within the self and the world, an element without which the question of God could not be asked. The unconditional is present in the theoretical realm as the *verum ipsum,* the true-itself, the norm of all approximations of truth, and in the practical realm, as the *bonum ipsum,* the good itself, the norm of all approximations of goodness. Such an experience of the unconditional element cannot be used, however, to establish an unconditional being within reality.

The Anselmian statement that God is a necessary thought and that therefore this idea must have objective as well as subjective reality is valid in so far as thinking, by its very nature, implies an unconditional element which transcends subjectivity and objectivity, that is, a point of identity which makes the idea of truth possible. However, the statement is not valid if this unconditional element is understood as a highest being called God. The existence of such a highest being is not implied in the idea of truth.[50]

Thus the ontological argument is true for Tillich, not as an argument which demonstrates the existence of God, but as the "acknowledgement of the unconditional element in the structure of reason and reality."

The traditional cosmological and teleological arguments for the existence of God are also an inadequate form of the question of God, and are valid in so far as they analyze reality in such a manner that they indicate the inescapability of the question.

It is impossible to argue from the endless chain of cause and effects to a first cause, for such a being would itself be a part of the causal chain. The notion of a first cause and of a substance are merely symbols determined by the structure of finitude. As

[50] *Ibid.,* p. 207.

such they express the question implied in finite being, "the question of that which transcends finitude and categories, the question of being itself embracing and conquering non-being, the question of God."

The teleological argument also simply formulates the question of the ground of meaning, and as such it is valid in that it shows that the question of God is implicit in the finite structure of being.[51]

The question of God is thus implied in the finitude of being, and since philosophy analyzes being, the theologian simply gives an answer to problems raised in a philosophical ontology.

Philosophy asks the ontological question: "What is being itself?" Tillich assumes that such a question is significant and can be answered meaningfully in a cognitive sense. For he seeks to discover what it is which is not a particular being or a collection of beings, but which is nevertheless at least implicitly presupposed and thought whenever something is said to be.[52] That ontology is possible is evident from the fact that ontological concepts exist which are less universal than being, but more universal than any concept designating a realm of beings. Such concepts are *a priori* in that they determine the nature of experience by constituting its very structure so that they are present whenever something is experienced. And yet such concepts are the products of an analysis of experience.[53] They are, moreover, not necessarily static in that experience may have changed in the past and may change in the future, but as long as there is experience, it will have an *a priori* structure which is recognizable.

Ontological concepts are of four different kinds, each of which demands a philosophical analysis and theological answer. The first level is concerned with the basic ontological structure implicit in the ontological question: the self and the world. The second deals with such elements which constitute the basic

---

[51] *Ibid.*, pp. 204, 210.
[52] *Ibid.*, p. 163.
[53] *Ibid.*, pp. 166 ff.

structure of being: individuality and universality, dynamics and form, freedom and destiny. The third deals with the characteristics of being which are the conditions of existence. And finally the fourth level deals with the categories viewed as basic forms of thought and being, e.g., time, space, causality, and substance.

Philosophical analysis on the first level discloses the basic ontological structure implicit in the ontological question.

As a neo-existentialist Tillich assumes that man is unique in that he is immediately aware of the fact that as a being, he himself participates in the structure of being, and that within himself all levels of being are united and accessible. The truth of ontology is thus dependent on the assumption that man occupies a peculiar position in ontology, since the ontological question can receive an answer by means of a human self-awareness, so that within man the principles of the universe are to be sought and to be found, since man has an immediate intuitive knowledge of the structure of being and its elements.

Ontological concepts on this first level are true to the degree that they are capable of expressing what makes the subject-object structure possible. Ontological concepts are attainable because of the experience that man has of belonging to a world from which he is distinct.

The experience of a self precedes all questions of existence. As a self, man has a world, a structural whole, and man's relation to the latter is the basic ontological structure which implies all others.[54]

The world is a structural whole; its structure is objective reason, the self is a structure of centeredness, subjective reason, and the relation between self and world, between subject and object is one of polarity. The basic ontological structure cannot be derived, so that only revelation can answer the question as to what procedes the duality of self and the world.

The second level of ontological concepts deals with polar elements constituting the ontological structure just described. An element of individualization is a quality of the ontological

[54] *Ibid.*, pp. 168, 171.

structure of being, a quality of everything. Individualization exists in polarity with the element of participation, so that individualization and participation provide the basis of the category of relation as an ontological element. The element of individualization guarantees the existence of things to be related, but without participation, the category of relation would lack a basis in reality.

Tillich's conclusions here as elsewhere are based on the existentialist presupposition that man is a microcosmos, a being within whom the world is directly present and consciously encountered. From the notion of a self, the notion of individualization is derived and extended to all of being, and from the alleged fact that man participates in the universe through the rational structure of his mind and of reality, the notion of participation is viewed as an ontological element, which guarantees the unity of a disrupted world, and makes possible a universal system of relations.

The polarity of individualization and participation enables Tillich to reject nominalism. For to hold that the individual alone has ontological reality, and that universals are simply verbal signs which point to similarities between individual things, is to overlook the fact that what is potentially a part of knowledge has the structure of being knowable, and such a structure presupposes a mutual participation of the knower and the known. Individuality and participation are elements of the structure of being, and the recognition of the participation of the knower in the known alone makes knowledge understandable. However, such a recognition need not embrace a second reality behind empirical reality, the error of Platonic realism; it need not posit a level of being in which individuality and personality disappear. For the element of participation belongs to the ontological structure of being, of the self, and the world.[55]

A second polarity of elements constituting the structure of being is that of dynamics and form. To be something means to have a form, and that which is formed by a form is designated

[55] *Ibid.*, pp. 174, 178.

by the term "dynamics," the potentiality of being, which is non-being, in comparison to things that have a form, and the power of being, in contrast to pure non-being. There is a dynamic element in the structure of being, a tendency of everything to transcend itself and create new forms. Becoming is a genuine element in the structure of being.[56]

Tillich also distinguishes a third element in the structure of being: freedom and destiny. In polarity with destiny, freedom makes existence possible in that it transcends the necessity of being without destroying being. Freedom is not a function of the will but of man, conceived of as a self. Destiny is the basis of freedom; it refers to all past decisions out of which present decisions arise. The polarity of freedom and destiny applies to all forms of being, to everything that is, although man is unique in experiencing freedom as deliberation, decision, and responsibility.[57]

It is now evident that Tillich assumes that philosophy is able to describe the structure of being in such a manner that its elements become intelligible. As an existentialist, Tillich assumes that man is able to look beyond the limits of his own being and of every other being. "He is free to transcend every given reality."

Tillich is not disturbed by the difficulties involved in asking the question of being. For the question of being is produced automatically by what he calls the "shock of non-being." But an appeal to the shock of non-being hardly seems adequate to justify a discussion of being. For if the significance of the question of being is called into doubt, an appeal to non-being can scarcely be of assistance. And yet Tillich is convinced that the question of non-being is unavoidable. For the notion of non-being cannot be restricted to the content of a logical judgment which denies a possible or real assertion, since every logical structure is rooted for Tillich in an ontological structure. Therefore, the notion of non-being cannot simply be a negative judg-

[56] *Ibid.*, pp. 178, 182.
[57] *Ibid.*, pp. 182, 186.

ment devoid of ontological significance. Logical denial presupposes being.

The unavoidable character of the distinction between being and non-being is supposedly evident from our awareness that certain expectations do not occur, and that erroneous judgments are possible when the conditions necessary for the expected event are non-existent. For the structure of being capable of accounting for the ability to transcend the given situation, and to commit an error, must include non-being.

. . . the very structure which makes negative judgments possible proves the ontological character of non-being. Unless man participates in non-being, no negative judgments are possible; in fact, no judgments of any kind are possible.[58]

The problem of non-being for Tillich is the problem of finitude, for the latter unites being with non-being, so that finitude is being limited by non-being.

Non-being appears as the not yet of being and as the no more of being. It confronts that which is with a definite end (finis). This is true of everything except being-itself—which is not a thing. As the power of being, being itself cannot have a beginning and an end. Otherwise it would have arisen out of non-being. But non-being is literally nothing except in relation to being. Being precedes non-being in ontological validity, as the word non-being itself indicates. Being is the beginning without a beginning, the end without an end. It is its own beginning and end, the initial power of everything that is. However, everything which participates in the power of being is mixed with non-being. It is being in process of coming from and going toward non-being. It is finite.[59]

Thus to be something is to be finite, so that under the conditions of existence, being is conceived of as finitude, which on the human level results in the experience of non-being as the threat to being. By looking at himself from the perspective of potential infinity, man becomes aware of his death and of his finitude in anxiety. For anxiety is not a psychological state but

[58] *Ibid.*, p. 187.
[59] *Ibid.*, p. 189.

an omnipresent ontological quality aroused by finitude, the threat of non-being.[60]

The last level of ontological concepts applies to the categories or forms with which the mind grasps and shapes reality, to the forms of being. The categories are ontological and are, therefore, found in everything and determine the content of what is experienced. The ontological character of the four main categories, time, space, causality, and substance is disclosed by their relation to being and non-being. As such they express being and non-being and they must be considered in relation to the world and to the self, for each category expresses a union of being and non-being and of anxiety and courage.

The central category of finitude is time which in self-awareness unites the anxiety of transitoriness with the courage of a self-affirming present. Through its union with space, time creates the present. Space is also an ontological category of finitude, since to be means to have space, and to be at the same time subject to non-being, since no finite being possesses a space which it does not lose.

As time and space, causality is also an ontological category in that it expresses being and non-being. Being is expressed by it in that it points to what precedes a thing or event as its source, and non-being is expressed since to speak of a cause of a thing is to admit that it does not possess its own power of being, thereby expressing the abyss of non-being in everything.

The category of substance also discloses its affinity with being and non-being by pointing to what underlies the flux of appearance and to the fact that apart from its accidents the substance is nothing.

Anxiety and courage are expressed in all the ontological categories; anxiety, in an awareness of finitude; and courage, in a willingness to accept finitude, an acceptance of the loss of being.[61]

Finitude is also expressed in the ontological elements as well

---

[60] *Ibid.*, pp. 189, 192.
[61] *Ibid.*, pp. 192, 198.

as in the ontological categories. And in the elements finitude also produces tension and anxiety, for the polar character of the elements creates a lack of balance, since a whole is not given. Individualization and participation, dynamics and form, freedom and destiny express their tension in the anxiety of losing our self and ontological structure by losing one or the other polar element.[62]

The essential nature of being is characterized by finitude in correlation with infinity. But in existence the unity of essential being is distorted and tension is again experienced.[63]

Philosophy is able to analyze the nature of being and to disclose the tension in its structure, elements and categories, but philosophy is unable to resolve the tensions implied in being. Tillich's entire analysis of being is, therefore, preparatory to the question of God. And on the basis of such an analysis he now feels in a position to resolve the problems (tensions) of being in a philosophical theology. For although philosophy is cognitive to the extent that it is able to disclose the ontological structure of being, it is not able to solve its own problems. On the one hand, Tillich ascribes a tremendous power to philosophy in that it can attain to metaphysical heights, but, on the other hand, in its correlation to theology, philosophy is unable to resolve its own alleged difficulties and must turn to theology.

Thus, although philosophy is capable of dealing theoretically with the structure of being, religion alone is capable of dealing with the meaning of being.[64] Consequently, the openness of being itself, as experienced religiously, is the foundation of the philosophical comprehension of the structure of being.[65]

The questions implied in the finitude of man and in the tensions of being can be answered solely in terms of God. The term "God" refers to what concerns man ultimately, and only that which concerns man ultimately is God for him. Ultimate

[62] *Ibid.*, pp. 198, 202.
[63] *Ibid.*, pp. 202, 204.
[64] *Ibid.*, p. 230.
[65] *Ibid.*, p. 235.

concern is beyond any finite, concrete concern.[66] What is of ultimate concern has the quality of being holy,[67] but everything secular can become the bearer of the holy.[68]

The idea of God is developed dialectically in the historical development of the various religions, so that the tension of the elements in the idea of God produces a stage in which the concreteness of man's ultimate concern results in polytheistic structures, whereas the absolute element results in monotheistic structures, and the desire for a balance culminates in trinitarian structures.[69] Trinitarian monotheism is not concerned with the number three; it is a qualitative rather than a quantitative description.[70]

God is being-itself, not a being along side of other beings, for he is not subject to the categories of finitude. He is the ground and power of being, the power inherent in everything, the power to resist non-being. As the power of being, God is beyond the contrast of essential and existential being. Being-itself does not participate in non-being. It is wrong to speak of him as existing. For the question of God's existence can neither be asked or answered.

Being itself is beyond every finite being, and yet every finite being participates in being itself, for otherwise it would not have the power of being and would be consumed by non-being.[71]

God is the ground and structure of being; the structure is grounded in him. God can be spoken of only in terms of this structure. To approach God cognitively is to approach him through the structural elements of being itself. Such elements make God a living God, the object of concrete concern.

The only nonsymbolic statement that can be made about God is that he is being itself. To speak of the actuality of God is to assert that he is not God if he is not being itself.

[66] *Ibid.*, p. 211.
[67] *Ibid.*, p. 215.
[68] *Ibid.*, p. 218.
[69] *Ibid.*, p. 221.
[70] *Ibid.*, p. 228.
[71] *Ibid.*, pp. 235, 237.

. . . God is being itself or the absolute. However, after this has been said, nothing else can be said about God as God which is not symbolic. . . . God as being itself is the ground of the ontological structure of being without being subject to this structure himself. He *is* the structure; that is, he has the power of determining the structure of everything that has being. Therefore, if anything beyond this bare assertion is said about God, it is no longer a direct and proper statement, no longer a concept. It is indirect and points to something beyond itself. In a word, it is symbolic.[72]

The religious symbol participates in the power of the divine to which it points. A concrete assertion about God utilizes a segment of finite reality to point to what is infinite, and such assertions can be made since everything participates in the infinite, in being itself.

It is the ontological structure of being as analyzed by philosophy which provides the material for the symbols which point to the divine life. To say that God is living is a symbolic expression which points to the fact that God is the ground of life.

Theology interprets the symbolic meaning of the previously described ontological elements and categories. And within the divine life, since God is being itself, every ontological element includes its polar element without tension and the threat of dissolution.

The elements of individualization, dynamics, and freedom are the source of symbolization of the relationship between God and man. They enable him to symbolize his ultimate concern in terms of his own being, as personal, dynamic, and free, so that God stands in analogy to what man himself is.

When Tillich speaks of a personal God, he is therefore not thinking of a completely perfect person who resides above the world and mankind. The protest of atheism is here valid. Personal God means for Tillich that God is the ground of everything personal, the ontological power of personality. He is the

---

[72] *Ibid.*, p. 239.

principle of participation as well as individuality, of form as well as dynamics, of destiny as well as freedom.[73]

All of the ontological elements are symbolized in the notion that God is spirit, the power through which meaning lives.[74] Each theological dogma is simply a further symbolization of the ontological structure of being.

For our purpose, however, it is not necessary to enter into the further details of Tillich's philosophical theology.[75] Our exposition of Tillich's attempt to relate philosophy to theology is now complete. It can be summarized as follows. In relating philosophy to theology, Tillich presupposes an intrinsic connection between two areas. Philosophy is, however, equated with ontology, with an analysis of being, an analysis of reality as such. And theology incorporates philosophy into its structure by utilizing ontology as the material out of which questions develop which receive theological answers.

[73] *Ibid.*, pp. 244, 245.
[74] *Ibid.*, pp. 249, 250.
[75] For a further critical treatment of Tillich's theology, see David H. Freeman, *Tillich* in International Library of Philosophy and Theology, Modern Thinkers Series, Presbyterian and Reformed Publishing Co. Philadelphia, 1962.

IV. Some Critical Comparisons

Our detailed exposition of the relationship between philosophy and theology, as exemplified in neo-Thomism, neo-Augustinianism, and neo-Existentialism, is now complete. The present chapter summarizes and gives a more comparative analysis of the positions elaborated. We shall restrict ourselves to selected topics which are crucial to the points of view under consideration. However, since our concern throughout has been to write a comparative study of the problem, within a specified framework, we shall continue to operate within these self-imposed limits.

Our criticism will, in the main, be internal criticism. We shall assume, at least for the sake of the argument, the basic presuppositions of the position under consideration, and we shall then seek to point out the difficulties and consequences of the view discussed. And to the extent that we engage in external criticism, criticism which depends upon presuppositions not acceptable to the philosopher whose views are under consideration, we shall limit ourselves to such presuppositions which are acceptable to at least one of the schools of thought dealt with in the first three chapters.

The Nature of Philosophy in Maritain, Gilson, Dooyeweerd, and Tillich

In opposition to Tillich, who holds that a Christian philosophy is a conflicting ideal, Maritain, Gilson, and Dooyeweerd hold that a Christian philosophy is an actuality. However, to the degree that they define the nature of a Christian philosophy, Maritain and Gilson are in basic disagreement with Dooyeweerd, and in apparent agreement with Tillich, in so far as the latter would maintain the autonomy of philosophy, and in so far as Dooyeweerd subordinates reason to faith.

We shall in this section seek to clarify the sense in which Dooyeweerd, Maritain, and Gilson speak of a Christian philosophy, and we shall make explicit Tillich's reasons for the rejection of a Christian philosophy.

Maritain and Gilson strongly insist that philosophy is autonomous and independent of theology, and yet what is true rationally cannot be in conflict with what has been revealed by God, and philosophy can, without recourse to faith, allegedly establish the existence and attributes of God, so that a harmony exists between philosophy and theology.

While formally agreeing with Maritain that philosophy is independent of theology, Dooyeweerd still insists that it is inseparable from religion.

The question is thus raised as to whether there can properly be any connection between religion and philosophy. If Christianity, for example, is a religion which purports to be the history of God's relationship to man, how can it be connected with a discipline which seeks to acquire a clear and distinct insight into the nature of human experience?

Gilson regards the problem of Christian philosophy as being twofold: Does the concept of Christian philosophy have any meaning, and has there ever been such a thing as a Christian philosophy?[1] The question is not simply whether there have

---

[1] E. Gilson, *The Spirit of Medieval Philosophy* (New York: Scribner's Sons, 1936), p. 2.

been Christians who also happened to be philosophers, but whether or not there can be an intrinsic connection between the Christian religion and philosophy.

The charge has been made by Brehier, for example, that the term "Christian philosophy" implies a meaningless contradiction and in addition there never has been an historical reality corresponding to the term "Christian philosophy."

Gilson and Maritain admit that religion and philosophy belong to different orders and that the essence of religion does not belong to reason; nevertheless, they contend that Thomism is in fact a Christian philosophy in its purest form;[2] and it is wholly rational; for no reasoning issuing from faith finds its way into its inner fabric.[3] Christian philosophy has in fact existed wherever the order of philosophy and theology has been kept formally distinct and Christian revelation has been accepted as an indispensible auxillary to reason.[4]

To disclose the influence of Christian revelation on the development of metaphysics is for Gilson proof of the reality of Christian philosophy.[5] The apparent inconsistency in affirming the existence of Christian philosophy rests upon the failure to distinguish the "nature" and "state" of philosophy; that is to say, what it is in itself, and the state it exists in real fact, historically, in the human subject.[6] The coming of Christianity has for Maritain and Gilson in no way changed the activity of the philosopher with respect to the object, principles and method of philosophy. The essence of philosophy is specified in terms of the object toward which it tends by virtue of itself.[7] And since it is concerned with the class of objects which are of their nature attainable through the natural faculties of the human mind, philosophy is an intrinsically rational form of knowledge, and philosophical wisdom is a perfect achievement of reason.

[2] J. Maritain, *Essay on Christian Philosophy* (New York: Philosophical Library, 1955), p. 30.
[3] *Ibid.*, p. 15.
[4] Gilson, *Spirit of Medieval Philosophy*, p. 37.
[5] *Ibid.*, p. 41.
[6] Maritain, *op. cit.*, p. 11.
[7] *Ibid.*, p. 13.

Whether in a pagan or a Christian mind, considered in itself philosophy depends strictly on natural or rational criteria, for the specification of philosophy hinges on its formal object which is wholly of the rational order. The designation Christian in the expression "Christian philosophy" therefore does not refer to that which constitutes it in its philosophic *essence.* Simply as a philosophy, Christian philosophy is independent of the Christian faith. But the term "Christian" in this context refers to the state or condition of its exercise. Philosophy does not in fact exist as an abstraction. Philosophy is a human activity; an activity engaged in by a concrete living personality, a personality who philosophizes with his entire personal nature, and not with a separate purely natural reason.[8]

While there is no such thing as a Christian reason, there is a Christian exercise of reason and there is no *a priori* reason to refuse to admit that Christianity has been able to change the course of the history of philosophy by opening new perspectives to reason.[9]

For the Christian philosopher reason alone does not satisfy reason, and Christian philosophy results when truth that is believed is transformed by reason into truth alone. The content of philosophy is, therefore, such rational truths which are discovered, safeguarded or explored with the aid of revelation.

Thus, even though Gilson agrees with Maritain that from the standpoint of its formal essence as philosophy, abstracted from all historical conditions of existence, philosophy is not Christian; he affirms with Maritain, nevertheless, that in so far as a Christian reflects on the content of his faith and discovers some beliefs capable of becoming the object of science, and if he owes this new philosophical insight to the Christian faith, he is a Christian philosopher.

Thus, in concrete historical reality, Christian philosophy constitutes for Gilson and Maritain one species of the genus philosophy and includes in its extension all those philosophical

[8] *Ibid.,* pp. 13 ff. Gilson, *loc. cit.,* pp. 36 ff.
[9] Cf. Gilson, *loc. cit.,* pp. 12 ff.

systems which existed only because a Christian religion existed and because philosophers were ready to submit to its influence.

Christian philosophy is thus to be sought in the state of philosophy. The Christian philosopher is in an entirely different position from the philosopher who does not acknowledge Christian revelation.

... The Christian believes that grace changes man's state by elevating his nature to the supernatural plane and by divulging to him things which unaided reason would be unable to grasp.[10]

Philosophy has thus benefited by grace and has been transformed into a Christian condition or state. Thus, as a result of Christian revelation, there are not only Christians who philosophize but the philosophy of such Christians is also actually Christian. To attain the highest truths reason requires assistance by an inner strengthening and the offering of new objective data. Human intelligence aided by grace has reached new heights and new achievements which are visible in the history of philosophy itself.

The objective contributions of Christian revelation to philosophy include in the first place such data which *per se* belong to the order of philosophy and which are knowable to reason, but which in actual fact went unrecognized by philosophers. Such data include the concepts of creation, of sin, of nature as being capable of being perfected by a supernatural order, of God as subsisting Being itself.[11] Secondly, Christian revelation confirms what philosophy already knew but concerning which there was an element of uncertainty. To the Christian, for instance, the validity of reason is divinely confirmed. And finally, the supernatural mysteries of faith are of importance to philosophy itself, since it can learn of divine things from faith and theology, and, by learning of the latter the experience of the philosopher is revitalized and he becomes aware of new problems.[12]

The subjective contribution of grace to the Christian philos-

[10] Maritain, *loc. cit.*, p. 18.
[11] *Ibid.*, pp. 19 ff.
[12] *Ibid.*, p. 23.

opher supports his natural reason and perfects his intelligence. Faith enables the philosopher to cling steadfastly to what he knows rationally. Thus, theology reinforces philosophical activity and faith and knowledge are united into a *solidité vitale,* which recognizes that the *sagesse theologique,* is far superior to the *sagesse des philosophes.* However, when engaged in its own pursuits, philosophy is free. It is not *serva* but *ancilla* of theology. Philosophy serves theology only when it is used by the latter to establish conclusions which are theological and not philosophical.

For Dooyeweerd, however, the problem as to whether or not the term "Christian" can properly be predicated of philosophy raises additional questions. Any attempt to decide the issue simply by showing that theology has or has not influenced philosophers does not touch the question as to the merit and extent of such an influence, and it does not provide a criterion to determine whether or not past systems influenced by a belief in revelation are philosophy or theology.

Dooyeweerd is not satisfied to use the term "Christian philosophy" to refer to a Christian state of philosophy. Dooyeweerd would transform the very essence of philosophy into a Christian philosophy, a philosophy which employs religious dogma in its inner fabric.

For Dooyeweerd, the problem of the nature of philosophy requires more than historical analysis. It requires a systematic analysis which determines the necessary conditions which make philosophy possible. The distinction between what philosophy is in itself and the state of philosophy is of little use unless it is possible to determine what philosophy is in itself.

The Role of Reason in Philosophy as Conceived of by Tillich, Maritain, Gilson, and Dooyeweerd

Tillich shares with Gilson and Maritain the desire to establish an intrinsic relation between philosophy and theology, a relation determined by the nature of the two forms of endeavor.[14] But Tillich's different conception of the role of reason and of

[14] Tillich, *The Protestant Era,* p. 83.

the nature of theology results, as we have seen, in a correlation between philosophy and theology in which philosophical analysis of the human situation gives rise to existential questions, the answer to which theology discovers in Christian symbols.

Gilson and Maritain seek to establish a harmony between reason and the Christian faith, and the latter includes a belief in a super-natural deity, a deity which Tillich rejects, since he accepts the criticism of naturalism with respect to any supernatural view.

Thus, whereas Gilson and Maritain employ reason to demonstrate the existence of God, thereby demonstrating a harmony between reason and the Christian faith, Tillich's use of reason leads to a symbolic conception of God.

It is, therefore, evident that while Tillich appears to share a common desire with Gilson and Maritain, a desire to establish a harmony between philosophy and Christian theology, Tillich is in fact hostile to any theology with objective content, and to any philosophy which claims to be able to do more than raise questions capable of receiving subjective answers.

By his refusal to reduce reason to the capacity for reasoning, Tillich assigns an ontological function to reason which enables the rational structure of the mind, subjective reason, to grasp and transform the rational structure of reality, objective reason. However, Tillich's conception of reason is not to be confused with the realistic doctrine that there is a knowable world of existence which man has not constructed.[15]

Tillich is of the opinion that "We transform reality according to the way we see it, and we see reality according to the way we transform it. Grasping and shaping the world are interdependent."[16] Nevertheless, the ultimately real is hidden so that reason must seek revelation.

To conceive of revelation as Gilson, Maritain and Dooyeweerd, as a super-natural self-disclosure of a personal God, is for

---

[15] Cf. John Wild, *Introduction to Realistic Philosophy* (New York: Harper & Brothers, 1948), p. 6.
[16] Tillich, *Systematic Theology*, p. 76.

Tillich a distortion of true revelation, for the latter does not mediate knowledge of otherwise unknown facts, but it opens a new dimension of understanding in relation to our ultimate concern.

For Tillich, the knowledge of revelation incorporated into the statements of theology is subjective, since revelatory propositions do not give theoretical information. Revealed knowledge is communicable solely to those who participate in it. Consequently the knowledge of revelation is independent of scientific theory and historical research.

Tillich's notion of revelation and of symbols is, therefore, not to be confused with the neo-Thomist acknowledgment that the essence of God is not fully known. For, as we have seen, although the essence of God is not to be apprehended, the divine attributes can be deduced, according to Gilson and Maritain, via negation from the fact that God is self-subsisting being. The names applied to God are for Tillich predicated equivocally, whereas for Maritain and Gilson they are analogically predicated, since the creature is causally related to God.

Objective truth concerning the existence and nature of God is, however, not accessible to Tillich. Tillich's God does not exist in such a manner that he can be objectively known to reason or via revelation.

Theology for Tillich can never deal with an object which is separate from our concern. The truth of theological propositions depends upon our subjectivity, upon the structure, meaning, and aim of human existence. Tillich's position is a form of Existentialism; it is preoccupied with what is a matter of being and non-being for us. In Gilson, Maritain, and Dooyeweerd man stands in a relation to God, so that the being of God is distinct from the existence of man. In Tillich, man is not created in the image of God, but God is created in the image of man.

The subjective or existential nature of Tillich's position is further evident from the fact that neither the historic creeds of the church, its authority, doctrine, or view of Jesus, or the Bible constitute for Tillich the norm of theology. Unlike Gilson, Maritain and Dooyeweerd, Tillich is not concerned with objective states of affairs but with the present situation of man, experienced in all realms of life in terms of conflict, self-destruction, meaninglessness, and despair. This experience produces the necessity of overcoming the divisions of our situation and of creating a reality which overcomes self-estrangement, produces reconciliation of man with himself. Such a reality Tillich calls the "New Being," Jesus as the Christ.

For Tillich God is, as we have seen, not a being, but he is an answer to the problems involved in an analysis of being. Ontological analysis is, however, analysis of individual subjectivity, since the self precedes all other structures. The principles of the universe are found within man. Thus, whereas reason in Gilson and Maritain demonstrates the existence of God, reason in Tillich raises the question of God.

For Tillich, what is revealed is not detached from our subjectivity, so that human existence determines what is revealed. Consequently, the content of revelation is in principle incapable of confirmation or disconfirmation by any historical evidence. Gilson, Maritain, and Dooyeweerd would agree with Paul that the Christian faith is based upon the resurrection of Christ from the dead, and that although no historical event could substantiate or confirm the redemptive efficacy of Christ's death and resurrection, historical evidence that Jesus never lived or rose from the dead would be sufficient evidence to refute the truth claim of the Christian religion.

Tillich's lack of concern with historical events discloses the subjective and irrational character of revelation, and thereby detaches the statements of theology from any historical framework. A theology detached from all contact with historical events and from all non-existential experience is, however, a meaningless abstraction to Dooyeweerd, Maritain, and Gilson, Gilson and Maritain would admit that one may reject the theology of Aquinas, but they would hold that at certain points, at least, such a theology is verifiable in the same sense that any other past event is verifiable. And it is at least possible to specify the conditions under which its historical statements would be true or false.

To Maritain, Gilson, and Dooyeweerd, Tillich's identification of the content of revelation with ultimate concern can only be viewed as a reduction of revelation to a subjective psychological state. For if revelation is never separate from the subjective act of receiving, it can never be regarded as something which is not the projection of a psychological experience. It may be possible to show that the notion of the ground of being, which is supposedly disclosed in revelation, exists in psychological experience, but what knowable structure other than a psychological state is referred to by the term "ground of being?"

Tillich assumes that a person is a possible bearer of revelation because he is able to participate in being itself, but what does the term "participate" refer to, and what change would occur in our experience, if it were not the case that a person participates in a structure which is supposedly distinct from a psychological state?

Dooyeweerd would agree that the term "participate" when used to refer to human experience is not able to refer to what lies outside of such experience. Tillich's usage of the term "participation" is metaphorical. To speak of a depth dimension of reality open to religious symbols, in which they participate, is to engage in speculative verbalization and to assume that there are entities which correspond to every linguistic form.

When Tillich speaks of the knowledge of revelation, he is therefore not concerned with ordinary knowledge about the structure of nature, history and man, but with a special kind of knowledge, a knowledge of the mystery of being. To use the term "knowledge" in such a manner that it refers to something which is in no way related to what is ordinarily understood by the term "knowledge" is at least confusing, and instead of assigning any cognitive significance to theology, it is an admission of the basic subjectivism of Tillich's system.

Tillich states that:

Knowledge of revelation, although mediated primarily through historical events, does not imply factual assertions, and it is therefore not exposed to critical analysis by historical research. Its truth is to be judged by criteria which lie within the dimension of revelatory knowledge. . . . The truth of revelation is not dependent on criteria which are not themselves revelatory.[17]

Such statements in Tillich clearly show that the "knowledge" of revelation does not make factual assertions. But if such is the case, why speak of knowledge at all? Why speak of revelation as the manifestation of the mystery of being for the cognitive function of human reason?

And what is of central importance is how is it possible to relate that which does not imply factual assertions to philosophy except by way of contrast? It is difficult to see how revelation can provide the synthesis of the dialectical polarities within the structure of reason when its assertions are non-factual. Of course, if the statements made by Tillich about the structure of reason are themselves non-factual, then the relation between reason and revelation simply relates two sets of verbal constructs to each other, both of which lack any basis in fact. And the statements of philosophy and theology are reduced to mere speculative verbalizations which may be of interest to the psychologist, but which are without philosophical consequences.

Tillich's conception of revelation, which allegedly solves the questions raised by reason, is from the standpoint of Gilson, Maritain, and Dooyeweerd, purely speculative. Its only criterion, namely, that a revelation is final, since it can negate itself without losing itself, is completely arbitrary.

By rejecting the authority of the New Testament, which Gilson, Maritain, and Dooyeweerd accept, Tillich can only answer philosophical questions in terms of a speculative theology. Tillich's construction of Jesus as the Christ is presented on speculative grounds, not on the basis of exegesis of the New Testament. The latter is interpreted in terms of a criterion which is imposed on the New Testament. Tillich's claim that

[17] *Systematic Theology*, pp. 130, 131.

Jesus accepted the title "Christ," on the condition that he would die and thus "deny the idolatrous tendency with respect to himself," overlooks the gospel account of the events surrounding the death of Jesus. For, the very reason for his execution was the fact that he claimed to be the Christ. There is absolutely nothing in the text to suggest that at his trial Jesus negated his historical existence. It was just this claim to be equal with God that brought about his execution.

One need not agree with Gilson, Maritain, and Dooyeweerd in accepting the claim Jesus made, but the New Testament clearly indicates that he made it. To interpret the New Testament in terms of modern existentialism is an unscholarly distortion of an historical document. Viewed from the standpoint of Tillich's own theology, we must formulate this distortion as follows: To make Jesus the perfect existentialist, a person in complete possession of himself, and transparent to the mystery of being, is to interpret the past in the light of the present. The application of existentialist categories to the past, in such a way that historical texts are distorted, is to forget that the categories of existentialism are of recent origin. Such a procedure is uncritical.

Tillich's view of Jesus as the Christ is the very opposite of that presented by the New Testament and is achieved by rejecting by means of an *a priori* criterion, the authority of everything finite in Jesus. What such elements include are known only to Tillich. The New Testament makes no such distinction.

Tillich's correlation of an arbitrary and subjective theology with philosophy thus results in a conception of philosophy which renders it incapable of attaining knowledge of non-subjective states of affairs. Consequently, although at first sight Tillich appears to agree with the neo-Thomists that philosophy and theology can aid each other, Tillich's conception of the role of reason and his subjective view of revelation betray on closer scrutiny a basic hostility to philosophy and to any theology that claims that its assertions refer to objective states of affairs.

It is also necessary to point out that Dooyeweerd, at least, is unwilling to grant that the mind is able to grasp and to transform reality. It is difficult to assign any meaning to the notion that reality is rational, if the term "rational" is used to refer to what is unexperienced, for the character of that which is not experienced is unknown. To speak of the rational structure of reality, therefore, is not to speak of a mysterious logos character of the world, but it is to speak of a quality of our experience, the quality of coherence. To describe the simple fact of coherent experience in terms of a correspondence between the rational structure of the mind and the rational structure of reality is, therefore, an unwarranted and unnecessary complication.

The mind and reality are not things related to each other, so that the rationality of each permits them to exist in correspondence. The term "mind" can also be used to refer to certain functions of human behavior. And "reason" may be regarded as a term which refers to certain forms of experience, to certain abilities and functions of the human organism.

If by the statements "reality is rational" and "the mind is rational" Tillich intends to postulate that there are actual and possible events, that there are existing states of affairs, some of which have been experienced by man, and that others probably will be, then such statements are harmless and rather trite. For to speak of a correspondence between a "rational reality" and a "rational mind" then simply means that there is something to be experienced, and something which has experience. But the notion of something to be experienced and of something which has experience is contained in the very concept of experience. Consequently, Tillich is in effect simply stating in a cryptic manner that experience is experience. And since no one is apt to deny that experience is experience, it is hardly worth pointing out, and certainly is not relevant in support of a speculative conception of "ontological reason."

Tillich has failed to demonstrate that there are states of affairs which necessitate a distinction between an ontological and a technical concept of reason. And it is difficult to see how the mind can be regarded as a static entity with a fixed structure enabling it to grasp and to transform another entity, namely, reality. The notion of reason may also be thought of as the capacity for reasoning, as a function or quality of experience, so that when Tillich speaks of reason in the philosopher grasping reason in nature, or reason in the artist grasping the meaning of things, or of reason in the legislator shaping society, the term "reason" in such contexts does not necessarily refer to a thing within the philosopher, the artist, and the legislator. It is not necessarily some mysterious property called "reason" which permits the philosopher, the artist, and the legislator to perform their tasks, but the philosopher, artist, and legislator may simply be regarded as human beings who follow a certain method in obedience to certain accepted norms. The term "reason" or "rational" may refer to their behavior, to their work, so that when behavior follows an accepted method and satisfies the desire for knowledge, beauty, or justice and security, then the behavior of the philosopher, the artist, and the legislator may be described as rational, in that it has followed a method which permitted the desired end to be achieved. The term "reason" in the expression "reason in the philosopher grasps reason in nature" may simply refer to the fact that the philosopher is a philosopher. The term "reason" in the expression "reason in the artist grasps the meaning of thing," may simply refer to the fact that the artist is able to be an artist, not because he grasps meanings, but because he satisfies the desire for beauty. And the term "reason" in the expression "reason in the legislator shapes society," may simply refer to the fact that the legislator is able to govern in a manner which satisfies the desire for justice and security.

And if reason is not an hypostatic entity with a subjective and objective structure, it is meaningless to speak of reason pointing to something which transcends it in power and meaning. That which has no independent existence cannot refer to its own depth. Consequently, if rational functions have no essential hidden qualities, then to speak of the "depth" of reason is to speak poetically, or prophetically, but while such language may be able to evoke certain emotions, it does not add to our knowledge or provide an adequate basis for the introduction of "myth" and "cult" into philosophical discourse.

Tillich is apparently unable to achieve a correlation between "reason" and "revelation," since in the context of his thought the term "reason" does not refer to any intelligible object.

To speak of actual reason moving through finite categories, through self-destructive conflicts, through ambiguities, in quest of what is beyond conflict and ambiguity, is to speak in a language which hypostatizes aspects of human behavior.

Tillich offers no conclusive evidence to support his contention that reason has structural elements capable of being in conflict. Methods may conflict, and hypotheses employed to explain sense data may differ, but to speak of a polarity between autonomous and heteronomous reason, a conflict resulting in the quest for theonomy, is to speak of distinctions which lack any corresponding basis in fact.

To be able to speak of the law of subjective-objective reason presupposes that the existence of the latter can be demonstrated, and that such a structure has a law character which is universally knowable. But Tillich does not first indicate how we know that there is a law of reason which is the law of nature within the mind and reality, a law rooted in the ground of being itself. To know such a law we would have to understand the structure of "the ground of being itself," but the expression "the ground of being itself," like "reason," "mind," and "reality," may simply be an hypostasis of experience.

The most basic presupposition of Tillich's conception of philosophy is a dialectical principle. In every area of investigation Tillich discovers a tension between opposites, a tension which is overcome in a synthesis in which the opposites are preserved.

It is the alleged polar structure of cognitive reason which leads to existential conflict and to the attempt to resolve such conflicts in revelation. The dialectical principle explains the ontological structure of knowledge, the distinction between subjective and objective reason, the conflict between autonomy and heteronomy, between the static and the dynamic, between the formal and the emotional.

Tillich's conception of philosophy is based upon a mystical experience, an immediate intuition of the unity of opposites. Such a subjective view of philosophy fails to establish that within the structure of the universe, unity is in fact ontologically prior to separation, so that reality is a dynamic process or movement, in which higher levels of synthesis are attained.

Tillich's intuition does not legislate what the structure of reality is. The dialectical principle assumes that the given meaning of a term embraces its opposite, but if such were the case, one could not ascertain the meaning of anything, including the dialectical principle.

Although Tillich refuses to admit that dialectics is in conflict with formal logic, he offers philosophy no safeguard against senseless combinations of words, and genuine logical contradictions. His only guarantee that dialectics does not genuinely conflict with formal logic depends on the acceptance of the very dialectical principle in question. For Tillich admits that in dialectics, yes and no, affirmation and negation, demand each other, whereas in formal logic, yes and no exclude each other, since (p) and (not p) cannot be true at the same time. And yet the introduction of dialectics is supposedly warranted because "dialectics follows the movement of thought or the movement of reality through yes and no." And since the movement of reality is described in logically correct terms which note the "intrinsic necessity which drives the old into the new," formal logic is supposedly not contradicted. But to assert that formal logic is compatible with dialectics, since the principle of dialectics adequately describes the movement of reality, is to avoid the problem and to assume that the nature of reality is known. An examination of the proposition "dialectics follows the movement of reality through yes and no," raises certain immediate difficulties. Is the proposition "dialectics follows the movement of reality through yes and no," itself subject to the dialectical principle? Or does the principle of non-contradiction apply to the dialectical principle itself? If the dialectical principle is designated by the letter (p), then can we say (p and not p)? Does the law of non-contradiction apply to p? If it applies, then at least p is not subject to the dialectical principle, so that p does not apply to all of reality.

To suppose that there is no contradiction between formal logic and dialectics in that the former expresses the static element in being, and the latter expresses the dynamic element, is to assume that the dialectical principle is warranted by the very structure of being. But that there is such a static and dynamic element in being presupposes that being is known via a dialectical principle.

The dialectical affirmation of opposites supposedly conforms to the principle of consistency because dialectics describes a movement. But as Demos correctly points out, Tillich intends to imply that:

The principle of contradiction maintains that p and not p cannot be true at the same time; but if the object of being described has moved, then p and not p may both be true of it because the contradictory propositions are referring to states of the object at different times. This is all true, but the analogy is made to apply to dialectical movement only because the word movement is used ambiguously. A physical movement takes time; but dialectical movement (the inner movement of the divine life) is timeless. In other words, the dialectical affirmation of yes and no is an affirmation *at the same time,* and thus violates the law of contradiction, the appearance to the contrary resting on a confusion in the use of the term movement.[18]

Genuine philosophy for Tillich supposedly begins with an ontological shock which expresses itself in the alleged basic question, that of being and non-being. And the distinction between being and non-being is thought to be necessary, for

... the fact of logical denial presupposes a type of being which can transcend the immediately given situation by means of expectations

[18] Raphael Demos, "Book Review of Tillich's Systematic Theology, Vol. I." *Journal of Philosophy,* Vol. XLIX, No. 21 (October 9, 1952).

which may be disappointed. An anticipated event does not occur. This means that the judgment concerning the situation has been mistaken, the necessary conditions for the occurrence of the expected event have been non-existent. Thus disappointed expectation creates the distinction between being and non-being. . . . Therefore, the very structure which makes negative judgments possible proves the ontological character of non-being. Unless man participates in non-being, no negative judgments are possible.[19]

But to base the distinction between being and non-being on unfulfilled expectation is to forget that expectation is a human attitude and as such can only refer to human psychology and experience.

Sidney Hook rightly protests that:

Expectation, however, is an attitude possible only to man. Where there is no man, there is no expectation, and therefore no non-being. Expectation, and therefore non-being, are purely psychological categories. We should therefore expect Tillich to admit that he is not dealing with a substantial force or power when he refers to "non-being." . . . Instead he forgets that he has just told us that human expectation has "created" non-being and maintains that man participates not only in being but in non-being. But one cannot participate in a distinction which one creates unless one, of course, is everywhere. . . . [20]

. . . Tillich's very language shows he has been misled by the *form* that a significant question has when it is asked about terms that have intelligible opposites, and uses the same *form* with words that have no opposites, and fails to see that when this is done, he has not asked a significant question.[21]

. . . Tillich is basing not only his ontology but his theology as well on a demonstrable logical mistake. There is no characteristic, to answer Tillich's question, which everything shows that participates in Being. An election, a table, a mirage, a pain, a stone, an idea, a power, a dream, a memory, an army, a geological stratum, . . . a corporation . . . have nothing in common except that they are ob-

[19] *Ibid.*, p. 187.
[20] Sidney Hook, "The Quest for Being." *Journal of Philosophy*, Vol. L, No. 24 (November 19, 1953).
[21] *Ibid.*, p. 718.

jects of discourse, or can be thought about. And "being mention-able" or "being thought about" is not a characteristic or property which belongs to anything in the way that triangular or human does.[22]

It is thus apparent that Gilson, Maritain, and Dooyeweerd agree in their rejection of Tillich's conception of the role of reason and its relation to revelation. It remains for us to show, however, that Dooyeweerd and Tillich are united in their rejection of the Thomistic arguments for the existence of God, although it is to be remembered that whereas Tillich rejects theism together with the traditional proofs of the existence of God, Dooyeweerd remains a theist, but bases the notion of the existence of God primarily upon his faith in the testimony of Scripture.

The Existence of God

Dooyeweerd and Tillich agree that the traditional proofs of the existence of God do not borrow anything from theology. But even if they are accepted as valid, Dooyeweerd and Tillich both contend that they do not guarantee that the God of the philosopher is identical with the God of the Christian theologian. The cause of the existence of every concrete object of experience need not be identical with the personal God of the Biblical religion.

The principle of causality upon which the neo-Thomistic proofs of the existence of God are based is supposedly known intuitively as an ontological principle. Dooyeweerd and Tillich agree that even if it be granted that there is a causal principle in the universe, it does not follow that such a principle is identical with an ultimate being which is outside of the universe.

Tillich accepts the view that the notion of the contingency of an object may imply that there is something upon which an object depends, but it does not imply that this something is not itself contingent. There is no reason why the many things of experience must have a single cause of their existence and not a

22 *Ibid.*, p. 719.

multiplicity of causes. And even if every finite series of things is causally related to some cause, all such finite series need not be related to a single cause which is not itself a part of the series. To search for the cause of all causes via an examination of being as being assigns a function to human thought which permits it to deal with what is beyond sensible nature. It assumes that the world of experience is analogous to what is not experienced directly, so that conclusions can be reached concerning what is beyond experience.

Dooyeweerd, at least, would find it difficult to see how the God of the Biblical writings who is concrete and personal can be identified with a concept of being, when the very term "being" is itself ambiguous. For example, it may serve as a copula signifying an implication, e.g., when the statement is made that "a concert is a musical performance"; or it may express an equivalence as in the expression "a dollar is a hundred cents"; or it may refer to the presence of a person, as in the expression, "he is here." But it is not possible to indicate how the term "being" can refer to a reality independent of experience, and to principles applicable to experience. The notion of being includes everything in such a manner that it lacks an element of differientation essential to a concept.

And even if we grant that whatever is moved in the physical universe is moved by a moving cause superior to it, and even if we accept the further assumption that the sufficient reason for the existence of individuals must be sought outside of the species, so that ultimately every instrumental cause is related to a first cause, it still would not follow that such a first cause must be identified with the personal God of Scripture. The cause of cosmic motion, and the cause of the existence of things is for Tillich and Dooyeweerd too easily identified by the neo-Thomist with the God of Exodus. For if God is conceived of as the first cause of an ordered series of causes, it is difficult to see how God can be distinct from the series, but it is also difficult to see how there can possibly be any room for ethical and moral freedom. To introduce the notion of human freedom, in a conception of the world which would ultimately relate all instrumental causes to an ultimate cause, appears most difficult; and yet the God of the Christian theologian presupposes moral freedom and human responsibility.

And at least Tillich would maintain that even if nothing now experienced in nature is necessary, it does not follow that nature itself is not necessary; what is now experienced as the natural world of things need not be transcended by a personal God. The natural order may itself be ultimate, so that the explanation of any particular thing may be given in terms of its relation to other natural things without assuming a supra-natural order, in terms of which the natural order is intelligible.[23]

And Tillich would admit that while it may be true that degrees of perfection are assigned to things because of the employment of a standard of perfection, it does not follow that there is a level of being which corresponds to distinctions that we have made. The assignment of degrees of goodness does not warrant the assumption that there is a personal God who is good. The notion of goodness need not exist outside the human mind. It is not necessary to assume that a personal God is the sufficient reason for the existence of things or the order of the world.

Dooyeweerd, on the other hand, would hold that the process of reasoning is able to examine meanings which have been assigned to terms and to form judgments about things which we experience, but it is not able to arrive at existential conclusions about that which transcends experience. That which is beyond the data of observation can be the object of religious faith, but not the proper object of demonstration.

The neo-Thomist is successful in meeting the criticism of Kant only if it be granted that the existence of a first cause is known from experience by means of an intuition of first principles. But the point in question is whether causality is related to being. Maritain and Gilson assume the very point which

---

[23] Tillich, *Systematic Theology*, Vol. II, pp. 5, 10.

Kant was unwilling to grant: that necessary realities correspond to necessary concepts of the mind.

Thomas would agree with Kant that God is not the direct object of our experience, but unlike Kant, Thomas defines knowledge in such a manner that God is knowable by analogy.[24] What God essentially is, is beyond our comprehension, but the manner of God's existence is knowable from what he is not, via negation.

The neo-Thomist holds that the concept of being is not applicable to God and to the creature in the same sense. It is an analogous concept. Our knowledge of God depends upon our knowledge of creation. If there was no similarity between God and the creation, then it would in principle be impossible for man to know God. It is the principle of causality that permits us to conclude, however, that there is a certain likeness between the creation and God. For since God is the first cause of the creation, the latter cannot be totally unlike God. There is, therefore, a proportional analogy between God and the creation; since God is the cause of things outside of himself, they resemble him as the effect resembles its cause. Thus, knowledge of God is acquired via knowledge of the creation. And it is precisely this conception of analogy that Tillich rejects.

This brings to an end our treatment of the relationship between philosophy and theology, as exemplified in three contemporary schools of philosophy. It is appropriate, in conclusion, to take cognizance of the widespread tendency to assume that theology is impossible because revelation is impossible, or because theological propositions are incapable of being formulated.

---

[24] Francis P. Clarke, "Kant and Thomas Aquinas on the Proofs for the Existence of God," in *Philosophical Essays in Honor of E.A. Singer, Jr.* (Philadelphia: University of Pennsylvania Press, 1942), pp. 315 ff.

V. Some Recent Objections to Theology

The introduction to the present volume pointed out that to establish the relationship between philosophy and theology, it is necessary to determine what philosophy and theology are. The absence of universal agreement as to the nature of philosophy makes it impossible to give a single definition of philosophy which is acceptable to all philosophers.

Whether the term "philosophy" is restricted to the logic of the sciences, or whether it is extended to include such questions as Dooyeweerd, Gilson, and Maritain discuss, is largely a question of definition. The fact remains that such questions are discussed.

Anyone who is unwilling to admit that certain propositions are different from the propositions of the separate sciences will be unwilling to recognize that there is a separate discipline which can be called philosophy. Whether a philosopher wishes to call such propositions logic, instead of philosophy is simply a matter of linguistic preference.

People do raise questions concerning God, man, and the nature of the world. Whether a person is willing to call such questions philosophical questions, as Dooyeweerd does, is again a matter of terminology. The type of question asked by Dooye-weerd, Gilson, and Maritain persist whether they are called philosophical or not.

The objection might be made, however, that the issue is not whether questions about God are to be called philosophical, theological, or religious; the real issue is whether it is possible to make any sense at all when we try to think and to speak about God.

The Problem of Religious Discourse

Some older forms of logical positivism simply ruled out the possibility of "religious knowledge" together with metaphysics.[1] It was thought to be absurd to state that "God exists" and equally absurd to state that "God does not exist," and until recently very little room was allowed for discussion. At present, however, there is considerable discussion of religious issues. The background of this discussion is provided by Alfred Jules Ayer's now famous book, *Language, Truth and Logic*. We shall begin, therefore, by stating Ayer's argument of 1936. We shall then briefly set forth certain more recent developments that have to a large extent been provoked by Ayer's original position.[2] And finally we shall offer a few critical comments which seek to justify the legitimacy of dealing with questions about God, and his relation to man and the world.

Ayer's original accusation that religious utterances are non-sensical stemmed from his general attitude toward metaphysics. The latter was to be disposed of, not by a criticism of the way in which it comes into being, but by a criticism of the nature of its statements.[3]

The metaphysician and, for Ayer, the theologian utter sentences which do not measure up to the standards which alone constitute a sentence as "literally significant." The condition

[1] Cf. Ayer, Alfred Jules, *Language, Truth, and Logic*, pp. 114 ff. Dover Publications, Inc. N.Y. 1946.
[2] Cf. E. L. Mascall, *Words and Images*, pp. 2-14, The Ronald Press Company, N.Y., 1957.
[3] Ayer, *op. cit.*, pp. 34 ff.

that every sentence must meet, if it is to be regarded as a significant proposition, is the criterion of verifiability in principle. A sentence is factually significant, if and only if, there are specifiable observations which warrant its acceptance as true and its rejection as false. Unless a sentence is a tautology, it is devoid of sense, if there is no observation relevant to the determination of its truth and falsity. Thus, for any proposition to be factual it must be an empirical hypothesis, i.e., it must be relevant to a future experience. Meaningful sentences either express tautologies or empirical hypotheses, but metaphysical sentences are neither tautologous, nor expressive of an empirical hypothesis; therefore, they are nonsensical.[4]

Any knowledge of God is precluded for Ayer, by his objections to metaphysical sentences in general. To those who would prove demonstratively that God exists, the question can be asked, What are the premises for such a demonstration? If the conclusion that God exists is to be certain, then the premises must also be certain, but if they are certain, then they are *a priori,* and if they are *a priori,* they are tautologies, and from a tautology, only a tautology can be deduced. It is not possible to deduce a statement about the existence of anything from an *a priori* statement, and an empirical proposition can never be more than probable. Ayer is, however, not willing to admit that it is possible to prove that God probably exists. If it were probable that God existed, the statement that he existed would be an empirical hypothesis, from which certain experiential propositions could be deduced. And since there are no such experiential propositions, it follows that God cannot be said to exist, even probably.

For Ayer, it is not meaningful to talk about God as a transcendent being, who although knowable through certain empirical manifestations, is, however, not to be defined solely in terms of such manifestations. Such talk is metaphysical talk, in which the term "God" is a metaphysical term, and statements about metaphysical terms are not genuine propositions. They

[4] *Ibid.,* pp. 41 ff.

cannot be true or false; they simply make no sense at all, i.e., they are nonsense.

Ayer believes his position to be incompatible with the atheist's and agnostic's position, as well as with that of the believer. For it is as nonsensical to assert that God does not exist as it is to assert that he does. A statement that lacks significance cannot be significantly contradicted. Even the agnostic makes the mistake of regarding the question as to whether or not God exists as a meaningful question, although he is not sure of the answer.

Some religious people may believe they can answer Ayer by agreeing with him that God's existence is not a matter of scientific proof. It might be argued that religion is a matter of faith in a being whose nature is mysterious, since God transcends our human understanding. But Ayer is not so easily put off, for he holds that to admit that something transcends the human understanding is to admit that it is unintelligible, and, if it is unintelligible, then it cannot be described significantly. Any truth about any matter of fact must lead to verifiable propositions, capable of being incorporated into a system of such propositions.[5] But for Ayer there are no religious sentences which meet his criterion of what is meaningful.

We shall return to Ayer's position, but first it is necessary to set forth certain additional objections that have been made against the possibility of *meaningful religious discourse.*

More Recent Developments

To most Christians it is reasonable to request that they be able to state what they mean and what they do not mean when they confess their faith.[6] Traditionally, when a Christian stated that he believed in God, he understood by "God" a being who is necessary, in contrast to all other beings, which are contingent. God is traditionally thought of as his own being, and his

[5] *Ibid.,* p. 120.
[6] Cf. The dialogue by A. N. Prior "Can Religion be Discussed?" in *New Essays in Philosophical Theology,* edited by Anthony Flew and Alasdair MacIntyre, Macmillan Co., N.Y., 1955.

own goodness. However, against those who hold that it is meaningful to state "God is his own goodness," the objection is raised that such a statement is simply bad grammar, a meaningless combination of words, because meaningful statements can be made, if and only if, the same word is not used as both an abstract and a common noun. It is quite legitimate to say either that "The people were very happy" or "The people's happiness was great," since both statements have the same meaning. But to say "God is his own goodness" is like saying "people are happiness!" The term "God" in the expression "God is his own goodness," appears to refer to a person or a thing of which qualities can be predicated, that is to say, the word "God" appears to be a proper noun. But to say that God is identical with that which is predicated of him is to use the same term as a proper noun and as an abstraction.

We can say nothing about God because we are unable to make sense when we talk about him. We are unable to attribute any quality to God *because of the limitations of our language.* It is not even possible to say that God exists, since existence is not a predicate that can be applied to things. To say something exists is not like saying that so and so has a property. For example, it is possible to say: Some cows moo, and to ascribe mooing to cows is to say something about them, but to say "Some cows exist" is not to say something about cows, it is simply to say "There are cows." To say "some cows do not moo" is clear, but to say, "Some cows do not exist" supposedly lacks any clear meaning.[7]

The reasons for stating there is a God allegedly presuppose that the term "God" refers to necessary being, whereas we can in fact speak solely of contingent beings. Existential statements are possible only with respect to what can be and not be. The notion of necessity can not be ascribed to anything which is. Propositions alone are necessary; things can never be necessary, any more than a square can be round.

It should at this point be clear that Ayer rejected religious statements as nonsensical primarily because they were metaphysical, while in recent discussion, certain writers have stressed the alleged impossibility of religous utterances due to the limitations of our language. This does not mean, however, that everyone has now abandoned Ayer's notion that a "sentence is factually significant, if and only if, certain observations would warrant its acceptance as true and its rejection as false. For it is possible to detect Ayer's influence at work in a recent discussion of the problem of *Theology and Falsification,* a discussion that occurred at Oxford in 1950-1951, and which is reprinted in *New Essays in Philosophical Theology.*[8]

The discussion was got under way by John Wisdom's article "Gods,"[9] in which a parable appears. The parable has been summarized by Antony Flew as follows:

"Once upon a time two explorers came upon a clearing in the jungle, in which were growing many flowers and many weeds. One explorer says, 'Some gardener must tend this.' The other disagrees, 'There is no gardener.' So they set up a barbed-wire fence. They electrify it. They patrol with bloodhounds. (For they remember how H.G. Well's Invisible Man could be both smelt and touched though he could not be seen.) But no shrieks ever suggest that some intruder has received a shock. No movements of the wire ever betray an invisible climber. The bloodhounds never give cry. Yet still the believer is not convinced. 'But there is a gardener, invisible, intangible, insensible to electric shocks, a gardener who has no scent and makes no sound, a gardener who comes secretly to look after the garden which he loves.' At last the skeptic despairs, 'But what remains of our original assertion? Just how does what you call an invisible, intangible, eternally elusive gardener differ from an imaginary gardener or even from no gardener at all?"

The parable as interpreted by Flew illustrates that what starts

[8] "Theology and Falsification" in *New Essays,* p. 96.

[9] Wisdom's paper was first published in the Proceedings of the Aristotelian Society, 1938. It is reprinted in *Logic and Language* (first series) edited by A. G. N. Flew, and in *Philosophy and Psychoanalysis,* by John Wisdom.

out as an assertion is finally qualified to such an extent that its qualifications reduce it to a "picture preference."[10]

Such utterances as "God has a plan," "God created the world," "God loves us as a Father loves his children" appear at first to be cosmological assertions. But to assert any proposition, P, is equivalent to a denial of its negation, not not-P. Whenever there is any suspicion that an utterance is not really an assertion, one way of putting it to a test is to ask what could count against the truth of the utterance in question. For an utterance is not really an assertion unless it denies something. An utterance which does not deny anything does not assert anything either.

For Flew, Wisdom's parable illustrates that the believer's original utterance was so qualified that it did not assert anything. Nothing could count against it. The believer who would assert, for example, that "God loves us" ought to be able to state what would have to occur to disprove that "God loves us." Flew would thus have the believer state what would be evidence against an assertion as well as what would be evidence for it. The believer is not simply asked to give reasons for his faith, but he is also asked to specify what would be evidence against his faith. Flew's question is, "What would have to occur or to have occurred to constitute for you a disproof of the love of God, or of the existence of God?"[11] The objection to religious utterances is that they are alleged to be compatible with every possible state of affairs. It is held that for an assertion to be an assertion it must make the claim that things stand in one way and not in another. And likewise any explanation must explain why a particular thing occurs and not something else.

Thus, whereas such older logical positivists as Ayer immediately ruled out theological statements as pseudo-statements, as nonsense, it is now fashionable to ask how theological statements are verified? What would confirm them and what would refute them.[12] The Christian may now be accused of holding

[10] *Ibid.*, pp. 97-99.
[11] *Ibid.*, p. 99.
[12] Cf. Basil Mitchell's "Introduction" in *Faith and Logic*, The Beacon Press, Boston, 1957.

two contradictory beliefs and of holding to both of them simultaneously, for he confesses his faith in a loving God while living in a heartless world.[13]

The Christian's utterances are held to be incapable of falsification, since all contrary evidence of the love of God, is simply qualified to the degree that nothing is allowed to count against God's love. The Christian refuses to recognize that every moral defect in the universe and every evil human act is the responsibility of God, since his omnipotence does not allow the Christian to say God would like to help, but cannot, and his omniscience does not allow the Christian to say that God would help, if he only knew. "Indeed an omnipotent, omniscient God must be an accessory before (and during) the fact of every human misdeed." . . .[14]

And yet for the Christian the statement that "God is love" is compatible with any state of affairs. No argument is allowed to count against it. As a result, religious statements are held not to be fully meaningful. For while they appear to assert that such and such is in fact the case, they are permitted to be compatible with any and every possible condition.[15] But utterances which do not mark out some one state of affairs are not really statements. In short, to know what something means implies that we know what it does not mean.

Thus to summarize what has been said, whereas Ayer rejected religious utterances because they were metaphysical, the present trend is to reject religious utterances either on the ground that the limitations of language do not permit us to assert them, or on the ground that they are incapable of falsification. It now remains for us to subject the positions surveyed to criticism.

Critical Evaluation

The older attack on religious statements, represented by Ayer, rejects such statements as "God exists" because they are

[13] Antony Flew, "Theology and Falsification" in *New Essays*, p. 108.
[14] *Ibid.*, p. 107.
[15] Cf. I. M. Crombie, on "Theology and Falsification" in *New Essays* pp. 109 ff.

metaphysical. The assumption is that any metaphysical statement is devoid of meaning because it is not verifiable.

It has been pointed out, that Ayer's original position would lead to the rejection of certain generalizations made in science, and that it has, therefore, been made the subject of criticism and has undergone modification,[16] so that it is now regarded by many as a proposal or definition. Ayer, himself, in the Introduction to the second edition of *Language, Truth and Logic*, admits that the verification principle is not an empirical hypothesis, but a definition, which is, however, not entirely arbitrary.[17]

Ayer is willing to distinguish between a "strong" and "weak" sense of the verifiable: "a proposition is said to be verifiable in the strong sense of the term, if and only if its truth could be conclusively established in experience, but that it is verifiable, in the weak sense, if it is possible for experience to render it probable."[18] Ayer now reformulates the principle of verification to be that any non-analytic statement that is literally meaningful must be directly or indirectly verifiable. It is directly verifiable if it is either itself an observation-statement, or is such that in conjunction with one or more observation-statements it entails at least one observation-statement which is not deducible from these other premises alone" . . .[19] It is indirectly verifiable if, in "conjunction with certain other premises it entails one or more directly verifiable statements which are not deducible from these other premises alone; and secondly, that these other premises do not include any statement that is not either analytic, or directly verifiable, or capable of being independently established as indirectly verifiable."[20]

By permitting the "other premises" to include analytic statements in the case of indirect verification, Ayer would make

---

[16] David H. Freeman, *Some Problems in Logical Empiricism*, Philosophia Reformata, 1953.
[17] Ayer, *op. cit.* p. 16.
[18] Ayer, *op. cit.*, p. 9
[19] *Ibid.*, p. 13.
[20] *Idem.*

room for scientific theories that do not designate anything observable. "For while the statements that contain these forms may not appear to describe anything that anyone could ever observe, a "dictionary" may be provided by means of which they can be transformed into statements that are verifiable; and the statements that constitute the dictionary can be regarded as analytic."[21]

Metaphysical statements are still excluded by Ayer because they "do not describe anything that is capable, even in principle, of being observed, but also that no dictionary is provided by means of which they can be transformed into statements that are directly or indirectly verifiable."[22]

Thus, Ayer's position in the second edition to his *Language, Truth and Logic,* is as hostile to what he calls metaphysics and theology, as was the first edition. However, his hostility is now more readily seen to be a fact about Ayer's preferences rather than a fact about metaphysical statements.[23] For Ayer now admits the necessity of detailed analyses of particular metaphysical arguments, if metaphysics is to be effectively eliminated, and he admits that his defense of the criterion of verifiability is the defense of a methodological principle.[24] But if such be the case, why must anyone else adopt Ayer's methodological principle? Mascall has correctly pointed out that Ayer's admission that particular metaphysical arguments need the support of detailed analyses, before they can effectively be eliminated, reduces the verification principle to a generalization from experience, and as long as some metaphysical propositions remain unexamined, it is possible that one of them may turn out to be valid.[25] Ayer now regards his principle of verification as a definition, and yet it is not arbitrary, or "it is not supposed to be entirely arbitrary." But why is Ayer's criterion not arbitrary? Mascall remarks: "For the assertion that the principle is a definition

[21] *Idem.*
[22] *Ibid.,* p. 14.
[23] cf. E. C. Mascall, *op. cit.,* pp. 7:14.
[24] Ayer, *op. cit.,* p. 16.
[25] E. L. Mascall, *op. cit.,* p. 9.

makes it impossible to question its truth, while the assertion that it is not entirely arbitrary suggests that some ground for its assertion is to be found in experience."[26] ... "Ayer rapidly oscillates between a number of positions, treating the verification principle at one moment as a definition, at another as a truth of logic and at another as an empirically verified generalization."[27] ... Mascall concludes that to be convicted of this, is to make Ayer guilty of what he condemns in others. For Ayer's basic doctrine rests upon "the absolute distinction between truths of logic and statements of empirical fact."[28]

The real reason why Ayer considers his verification principle not to be arbitrary is that the verification principle is a deduction from Ayer's basic assumption that what is meaningful is in the last analysis to be derived solely in terms of some form of human experience. By secularizing the Christian doctrine of creation, man alone is thought to be the creative source of meaning. Man is freed from any obligation to recognize his creaturehood, and what is not the creation of his own theoretical activity is at most regarded as probable.

Ayer absolutizes two special forms of scientific thought, the logical, and psychological. It is for this reason that he brands as meaningless any statement that is not a tautology or which is not directly or indirectly related to an observation report. This restriction of experience to what is directly or indirectly observable makes man's observations the origin of what is meaningful. It is itself the absolutization of an aspect of the fullness of our experience. The world exists whether it is experienced or not. It is not our observation of the world that makes it what it is, but it is what the world is that makes it possible for us to know it.

A truly "empirical" approach to any object employs a method that is suitable to the nature of that object. To assume that the only method that will yield knowledge is the method of observa-

---

[26] *Ibid.*, p. 8.
[27] *Ibid.*, p. 9.
[28] *Ibid.*, p. 10.

tion, assumes that to be knowable is to be directly or indirectly observable. Such an assumption rules out the possibility of our knowing anything about what is not so observable. It fails to take into account the nature of theological statements. For in the case of Christian theology, they are statements that occur within the aspect of faith. Their norm is not to be found in their verifiability in Ayer's sense, but in their conformity to the revealed word of God. Admittedly their truth is not demonstrable by an appeal to a present observable event. They are rather that by which the religious significance of all observable events are interpreted. To say that the statement "God exists" is meaningless because we cannot point to "God," simply begs the question. It assumes that what we can point to, i.e., the world, is ultimate, and that our experience legislates for what actually is, or at least what is knowable.

Ayer's own position, while pretending to be anti-metaphysical, is itself metaphysical. It presupposes that there is nothing, at least nothing knowable, that is not identical with some aspect of the natural world. Ayer rules out theological statements, because he has ruled out a God that ultimately justifies them. Statements about God are meaningless for Ayer because Ayer believes that what is meaningful must ultimately derive its meaning from man.

Ayer's position rests upon an *a priori* of faith; an *a priori* which, in apostasy from the God of revelation, places its trust in man's own sovereign personality.

We have not tried to show that the content of Ayer's faith is false. It is sufficient here to show that Ayer's principle of verification is not a "neutral," "philosophical" or "scientific" assumption; it is rather a "dogma" that Ayer happens to share with many others, a dogma which fortifies Ayer's religious conviction that "thou shalt have no other gods higher than Ayer," thou shalt not bow down to them, nor serve them, for the dogma of human autonomy is a jealous "God," and all statements about other gods are meaningless.

Much that has been said about Ayer is also true of the more

recently alleged impossibility of religious statements due to the limitations of our language.

A theory of language does not occur in a vacuum, and the theory of language that refuses to admit the possibility of statements about God presupposes a particular view about the origin, nature, and the purpose of language, which in turn rests upon a view of man, the world in which he lives, and the origin of the world.[29]

Either man is a creature of God or he is not. If he is not, then it makes no sense for man to utter statements about a non-existing creator. But if man is a creature of God, then he was created by God with the power of speech that is adequate for man to express his faith.

Gordon Clark deals with this problem by stating: "If God created man in his own rational image and endowed him with the power of speech, then a purpose of language, in fact, the chief purpose of language, would naturally be the revelation of truth to man and the prayers of man to God" . . . "language was devised by God, that is, God created man rational for the purpose of theological expression. Language is, of course, adaptable to sensory description and the daily routine of life, but it is unnecessary to invent the problem of how sensory expressions can be transmuted into a proper method of talking about God."[30]

We need not fully agree with Clark that language has a chief purpose, but we can agree that it is unnecessary to invent the problem as to how "sensory expressions can be transmuted into a proper method of talking about God." Such a difficulty arises when the linguistic aspect, together with sense perception, is absolutized and made the common denominator for all experience, so that the aspect of faith, in which religious utterances are made, is reduced to a matter of linguistics and sense experience.

[29] cf. Gordon Clark, *"Special Divine Revelation as Rational,"* In *Revelation and The Bible*, p. 40, edited by Carl Henry, Presbyterian and Reformed Publishing Co., Philadelphia, 1958.

[30] *Ibid.*, p. 41.

It is of course true that when a Christian confesses his faith he does not give an exhaustive, precise, scientific definition of God, a definition in which all mystery is removed. Some Christians, at least, have always held that, while there is no mystery in God, our definitions of God do not exhaust his inner nature. The assumption that we can say nothing about God because we cannot say everything begs the question. For when we confess our faith we do not claim that we exhaust God in our definitions. Our language is admittedly inadequate to express fully the nature of God. The God of the Bible can never be fully known by philosophical analysis. If we worship the Biblical God, then the God whom we worship is not fully comprehensible, philosophically. We must recognize that the very attempt to make God fully comprehensible, is itself equivalent to a denial of the Biblical God.

In other words, if the Biblical God is God, then He is not fully known. Thus any God that is fully known, is not the Biblical God. It has been correctly said that no creature can know all that is proper to God and no creature can give an exhaustive statement of all that God is.

The Christian does not claim to comprehend fully both the essence and the attributes of God; nor does he claim to know exhaustively all of God's attributes, nor to understand fully the relation in which these attributes stand to God, and the way in which God is related to the world.

The Christian admits that his knowledge of God is imperfect and yet he believes it is true as far as it goes. It has been well said that God is what we believe him to be, so far as our idea of him is determined by the revelation which he has made of himself in his works, in the constitution of our nature, in his word, and in the person of his Son.

And yet even when the Christian exercises the proper caution, his attempt to speak of God does not go unchallenged. For if he says that God is a spirit, infinite, eternal, and unchangeable, in His being, wisdom, power, holiness, goodness and truth, he may still be told that such a statement is bad grammar, a meaningless combination of words, like round square, cat no six, all mimsy were slithy toes and the mome raths outgrabe.

We are not simply told that the statements that we make about God are false, we have become accustomed to this; we are told rather that the attributes that we ascribe to God are pseudo-concepts, and the statements or judgments that we make about God in which such concepts appear are pseudo-judgments.

Let us try to gain some deeper insight into what is here meant. If I say, "This table is green," when in fact it is not green, the term "green" is not a pseudo-concept and the judgment, "This table is green" is not a pseudo-judgment; it is simply false. For while this table is not "green," the notion of "green" is a property which can be ascribed correctly to other states of affairs, such as grass. In fact, if we were to state that "the square root of 6 is very red," even though such a statement is preposterous, it would still not be a pseudo-statement, since some other things are very red.

If the propositions of theology are pseudo-propositions, then theologians must be very confused indeed! For while they think they are making sense, they are in fact simply giving vent to feelings and attitudes, which they express in combination of words that have no meaning.

Our objection to such criticism is the simple answer that questions of existence are prior to questions of the meaning of words. The rules of grammar describe the way in which we speak in a given language, they do not determine *what is.*

There may have been a time when there was no human speech, and yet there were things that could have been described, if man had been present; obviously man's description does not constitute the nature of things.

A normal infant comes into the world with the potentiality of speech, and it reaches a stage in its development where it is capable of making any basic sound that a human being can make. From this point it goes on to imitate and learn the meaning of words, but its ability to speak, and the limitations of whatever language it learns has no bearing upon the nature of the world. Likewise, man as such has entered a world that he did not make. And either this world of space and time is all that there is, or it is not. Either this world is "God," or it is not. God is the world, or he is not. And, the decision that is reached here is prior to any questions concerning our ability to describe God adequately.

When we say that "God is his own goodness," we confess our faith in a being beyond the contingent finite realm of cosmic time. To say that "God is his own goodness: is not to give an exhaustive definition of God. Admittedly, our language is inadequate to describe God fully. Negatively, at least, the meaning of the expression is clear—we mean that there is no standard or source of goodness—no Platonic realm—upon which God is dependent, i.e., God is really God. The term "God" refers to that which is beyond our temporal world, to that which is the origin of all that we experience as temporal. The rules of grammar apply to a segment of human experience; they do not legislate for the universe.

Language ought not to be confused with reality. Either God exists, or he does not. If God exists, then he exists prior to and independently or our ability to signify what he is.

The nature of the universe could only depend upon our ability to express it, if man were himself God. But our words are not The Word. The Word, who became flesh is not subject to our words; the reverse is true, our words, and our rules of grammar ultimately depend upon the Word that has dwelt among us, for it is He that hath made us, and not we, ourselves.

This brings us to our final criticism. It concerns the objection to religious discourse on the ground that religious statements are not capable of falsification, and are not assertions at all. Wisdom's parable is supposed to show that the believer qualifies what he asserts to the point that he does not assert anything.

In our judgment the demand that a religious statement be capable of immediate falsification in terms of immediate experience completely distorts the very nature of a religious statement, such as "God is love." To meet this objection, we must ask when a statement is properly qualified by the adjective religious. It might appear that any statement dealing with the religious experience of a person is a religious statement. But statements about religious experience, while they may presuppose religious statements, are not themselves religious. To the degree that a statement is the subject matter of biology, psychology, sociology, the science of history, or any other science, such a statement is not religious. A proper religious statement is qualified in the pistical aspect of experience, i.e., it depends in the last analysis solely on our faith. Its norm is the revealed Word of God, the Holy Scriptures. It has no other source by which it can be verified or falsified.

Religious statements are justified solely in terms of a person's most basic presupposition concerning the origin of everything we experience, i.e., the origin of the world, of ourselves, of what we are, and what we ought to become.

A statement is religious when it refers to, or is based upon the commitment that a person makes to whatever he holds to be "God." A person may not be fully conscious of the religious statements to which he holds, but upon questioning, it is in principle possible to bring his basic religious presupposition to the surface. To use a simple illustration, if we examine an everyday object such as a chair, we can regard it from many points of view, e.g., its economic value, its aesthetic qualities, its physical chemical properties, its effect upon society, its influence upon our feelings and behavior, and so on, but we can also ask whether this chair exists as a part of an all-inclusive system of nature, which sets its final limits, or does it ultimately owe its origin to a creator beyond the cosmic temporal order? The way in which such a question is answered, or dismissed, involves religious statements, which in turn rest upon a person's faith.

A further characteristic of a religious proposition is that its truth or falsity is not capable of being decided by a limited appeal to the senses. Statements used in support of religious statements may in principle be open to a direct and immediate test, but genuinely religious statements are not.

For example, Paul mixes religious statements with historical statements. When Paul states that three days after his death, Jesus "was seen of above five hundred brethren," Paul's statement can be checked in principle, but when he goes on to connect the death and resurrection of Jesus with the forgiveness of sin, and the final conquest of death, and when he elsewhere (Philippians 2) identifies Jesus with a pre-existent being "Who, being in the form of God, thought it not robbery to be equal with God" ... and "was made in the likeness of men," then such statements are, in principle, beyond what is immediately verifiable by any direct test.

Now since a genuine religious statement is not verifiable by any direct test, anyone who equates the meaning of a proposition with the method by which it is put to an empirical test, will dismiss religious statements as lying outside the domain of what can be true or false. They will deny that they are assertions. But such a denial is, as we have seen, a deduction from a naturalistic assumption, and in the last analysis is the result of a humanistic *a priori* of faith.

It is to be noted, however, that it is not verifiability to which the Christian objects. That "God exists," that "He is love," are statements that are verifiable after death. What is objectionable is the requirement that such statements, which refer to what is beyond the cosmic law order, be verified here and now in terms of temporal experience.

The Christian philosopher or theologian is not afraid of verification, but his religious beliefs will ultimately be verified when we meet Christ, face to face, and there is nothing that can happen to him here on earth that can shake his faith in the love of God, which is in Christ Jesus our Lord, neither distress, persecution, nor powers, nor things present, nor things to come, nor "contemporary philosophers."

The Problem of Revelation

Our preceding analysis of Tillich's position is sufficient to indicate that theology is possible as a science, if and only if, it has some data to investigate. Tillich's "theology" is an example of spinning ideas out of one's own head.

Theology has something distinct to investigate if, and only if, there is in fact a revelation from God to man. Many moderns, including Tillich, apparently assume that such revelation is impossible. Are there any reasons for this assumption? Is this simply an *a priori* of faith, a dogmatic postulate, or an unproven assumption from which one can deduce that all claims to the contrary are false? Or are there any grounds for this assumption?

What would someone need to know in order to assert with certainty the proposition "Revelation is impossible"? Remember that this proposition not only denies the actuality of revelation, but it also denies the very possibility of it, thereby precluding further investigations into all claims that revelation is actual.

We have seen in our introduction what conditions would need to be met to establish the actuality of revelation. From our analysis it is readily evident that revelation would be impossible if in fact there was no God (X) who knows something (S) and has purposes (P) and is capable of employing means (M), at a certain time and place (T) to make (S) known to man (Y).

Whatever is impossible is absurd, and whatever is absurd is impossible. What is it that makes something absurd? Something is absurd, if and only if, it is intrinsically contradictory. Such a situation is reached when the same proposition is simultaneously asserted to be true and to be false. It would be absurd to assert that God exists and God does not exist. It would be absurd to assert that God knows something and God does not know something. To assert God has the means and the purpose to make something known to man and God has no means and no purpose to make something known to man, is absurd. And whatever is absurd is impossible, and conversely. Revelation, in our sense of the term, would be impossible and therefore absurd if either God did not exist, or he had no purposes, or he did not have the means, or the knowledge (S), to disclose to man.

The person who asserts "Revelation is impossible" either knows what he asserts or he does not know it. The word "know" may be used in a way that is synonymous with faith. I may say I know something when what I mean is that I believe it with psychological certainty. If when someone asserts that he knows revelation to be impossible, he simply means that he is psychologically convinced that revelation is impossible, then he is doing little more than disclosing something about his own personal state of mind. He is confessing his faith!* However, "know" may be used to stand for what one holds to be true on the basis of conclusive evidence. Now what type of evidence, would a person have to "know" in this second stronger sense that revelation is impossible? If someone knew that God did not exist, then he would know that revelation is impossible. But what conclusive evidence is there that God does not exist? Unless someone has conclusive evidence that God does not exist, he cannot know with certainty that revelation is impossible. He may believe whatever he wishes, but what a person believes and what he knows are not necessarily identical.

Propositions that have God as their subject are religious and/or metaphysical propositions. To assert that God exists or to deny that God exists is to assert a religious and/or a metaphysical assertion. The evidence that is relevant to the establishment of the truth or falsity of such assertions must, therefore, be religious and/or metaphysical assertions. In any case, it should here be evident that to know that revelation is impossible is not easy. Anyone who thinks he knows this in the strong sense of "know" thinks that he knows quite a bit. For he claims to know the very nature of the universe. He knows that there is nothing capable of making anything known to him by any means. He also knows that all claims that people have made that such disclosures have taken place are in fact false claims.

---

* It will subsequently become clear that the term "faith" is used in more than one way. It sometimes stands for what we believe in the absence of evidence, the weaker sense, and at other times it stands for what is believed on the basis of partial although *adequate* evidence. We are here using the term in its weaker sense.

Revelation is admittedly impossible unless there is a God that is capable of knowing and of having purposes. Frequently what lies behind the tacit assumption that revelation is impossible is the assumption that a personal God is impossible.

Many people today still use the term "God," but they use it to designate the totality of things that constitute what is ordinarily called the material world. "God" is used synonymously with "nature." Or the term may be used to stand for the sum total of human ideals. It then becomes apparent to many that while man becomes aware of nature or of his own ideals, nature and ideals do not become aware of him. An act of revealing can take place solely between persons; so, if within the universe man alone is capable of purposive behavior, then man alone is capable of revealing.

The rejection of revelation here rests upon the metaphysical assumption that everything other than man is impersonal. The extension of the concept of a person is limited to man alone.

When it is said that man is a person, what is meant among other things is that man is capable of conscious purposive, intelligent behavior. To be a man is to be a person. It is to be aware of one's self and to be aware of others. A person is conscious of himself and of the world in which he lives. He functions in every aspect of his world. A person exists under the same physical conditions as does a stone. The concepts of the physicist can be applied to both man and the stone. But this does not imply that men are stones or that stones are men. The difference between man and a stone is partly expressed by the term "person."

The biologist is also able to describe man and animals in certain common terms. They share certain functions from a strictly biological point of view. Because men share certain biological functions with animals, it does not follow either that animals are men or that men are animals. Men defecate and animals defecate, but this does not mean men are animals. And what makes man different from the animal is partly expressed by the term "person." It is precisely the fact that man is a personal being that enables him to state that he is an animal. I know of no animals that have claimed to be men.

What makes man a person is not that he has such feelings as pleasure and pain, but that he is aware of such feelings; he can study them, form concepts about them, and subordinate them to his plans and purposes.

What makes man a personal being is that he can freely transform his physical environment into a civilization, constituted by government, art, science, language, law, religion, and a wide variety of groups and purposive associations.

In brief, to conceive of man as a person is to conceive of a wide variety of free, conscious, purposive behavior traits. It includes man's knowing, planning, conceiving, and many other aspects. The essential characteristic, however, is the element of self-conscious, purposive activity, i.e., when someone acts as a person, he is aware of himself when he acts, and in general he knows why he acts; he has a purpose.

Now when it is said that God is a personal being, what is meant in part is that God acts in a personal way, so that while God cannot act in a way that would be contradictory to his own nature, yet he can act in a conscious, purposive manner.

It is precisely at this point that the objection might be made that what makes revelation impossible is the fact that personal beings alone are capable of performing acts of revealing. And since God is not a personal being, God is not capable of performing acts of revealing. We have argued in support of the major premise, that personal beings alone are capable of revealing. And if the minor premise is granted: that God is not a personal being, the argument would be sound. It is precisely the minor premise, however, that begs the question. That "God is not a personal being" is the very point of contention.

In support of the minor premise it might be argued that the very notion of a personal being is derived from human experience and is to speak of God in human form. While it may be acknowledged that there is some power or force in the universe that may be called God, yet to speak of God as a personal being is to ascribe human traits to what is admittedly infinite and beyond all human limitations.

The preceding argument undoubtedly objects to the tendency that many have to conceive of God in terms similar to Michel-Angelo's painting, as an old man with a beard. Those who would conceive of God as a force, however, often forget that the notion of a force or power also originates in human experience. There is the danger of thinking of God as an old man, but there is also an equal danger that one might begin to think of him as electricity. What purports to be a more modern sophisticated view simply becomes the deification of nature. There is certainly nothing new and modern in this procedure.

There are many reasons for the widespread acceptance of the premise that God is not a personal being. If we were to venture a guess, however, it is probable that the rise of secular education has produced the phenomenon that otherwise well-educated people are childish in their understanding of what theologians are trying to say.

It is not uncommon to encounter a person who has distinguished himself in a non-theological field, who rejects or accepts religious beliefs on the level of comprehension possible to a bright eight-year-old child. There is no difference between the religious views of the child and the adult in such a case. However, there frequently is a difference between their respective attitudes. The child is bright and alert; he knows that he is growing up, and is therefore inquisitive and open to new interpretations. He is filled with questions. But the adult with childish beliefs still acts like an adult. He is psychologically as certain of his childish beliefs as he is of his mature judgments, and he is often completely unaware that there are those who have gone beyond the level of a child in religious matters. The rejection or acceptance of a personal God is immature if a person does not understand what it is that he is asked to accept or to reject.

Few, if any, Biblical theologians have ever conceived of God in a crude literal fashion. There is something peculiar about religious language. For example, the reader may remember the Old Testament account of the occasion when Samuel appeared before King Saul to rebuke him for his disobedience. In 1st Samuel 15, verses 10, 11, we read "Then came the word of the Lord unto Samuel saying, It repenteth me that I have set up Saul to be king" . . . and in verse 35, we read . . . "and the Lord repented that he had made Saul king over Israel" . . . And yet just a few verses before in verse 29, we read "And also the strength of Israel will not lie nor repent: for he is not a man, that he should repent."

It would be easy to dismiss these verses as hopeless contradictions. Anyone unfamiliar with Biblical exegesis might simply hold that the author here affirms that God repents and God does not repent. It is, however, reasonable to ascribe as much intelligence to the author of such a narrative as we would like to have ascribed to our own efforts at communication. The simple and obvious explanation is that the word "repent" is being used in more than one sense. The negative statement that Goes does not "repent: for he is not a man, that he should repent" is meant to be literal. For it fits in with the Old Testament portrayal of God. The statements that the Lord "repented" that he made Saul king are more difficult to understand. They are, however, not to be taken univocally, i.e., the writer is not here ascribing human emotions to God in a strictly literal sense.

The popular misconception that the God of the Old Testament is a crude tribal deity, who is vengeful, fickle, and fearsome, while the God of the New Testament is a God who is meek and mild, is in part due to a failure to give due consideration to the nature of the language used within the Biblical text.

All language that man uses is human language. And when man speaks of God, he must speak as a man. Likewise, if it is the case that God has in fact revealed himself to man, the means that he uses must be such that man could understand what God would have him understand.

It is not necessary to go into all the implications and exegetical difficulties in the statement that the Lord repented that he made Saul king over Israel. Verse 29 makes it obvious that Samuel clearly does not intend to ascribe any activity to God that is contrary to the divine nature. Repentance when ascribed to God differs from human repentance as the divine nature differs from human nature. Samuel may be saying no more than that Saul's behavior is contrary to what God would have him do, and that the consequence of his disobedience was to be his downfall. Much more may be implied. In any case Saul knew more about God after Samuel left him than he did before.

Many modern intellectuals erroneously feel that they are in the grip of the following dilemma. If a person speaks of God literally, then the result is a crude primitive theology which is absurd. If a person does not speak literally about God, then the result is a scepticism that entails the rejection of a personal, revealed being. And since a person must either speak of God literally or not speak of God literally, he must either accept an absurd primitive theology, or he must accept a scepticism that entails the rejection of a personal, revealed being.

The force of this dilemma lies in its formal validity, but it can readily be rebutted by an equally valid counter-dilemma: If a person speaks literally about God, then this will not lead to scepticism, and if a person does not speak literally, then this will not lead to absurdity. And since we must either speak literally or not speak literally of God, we either do not end in absurdity or we do not end in scepticism. The choice between speaking literally and speaking analogically may not be quite so simple as the preceding dilemmas suppose. It may be that when a person speaks literally about God, he speaks analogically. What is said of God is not always meant to be entirely literal, nor is it meant to be wholly non-literal. It may be that sometimes when a person speaks about God, there is an element in what he says that is literal and an element that is also analogical in a proper non-metaphorical sense It might then be argued that, sometimes when a person speaks literally and analogically about God, he does not speak absurdly. But what is meant by speaking analogically? There is much that could here be said and there are many distinctions that could be made.[31]

Suppose, for example, one were to say that the lion is to the beasts of the field as the King of England is to the people of England. Such an ascription of kingship or dominion to a lion is hardly to be taken literally. There is no sense in which a lion is really a king. And yet the metaphorical use of kingship, when applied to a lion, gives some indication of his strength, grace, and beauty. Nevertheless there is not much likeness between a lion and the King of England.

Suppose, however, one were to say that a chair has arms and a man has arms. In what sense could one then speak of the ascription of arms to a chair and the ascription of arms to a man as being analogical? Obviously the arms of a chair are not the same as the arms of a man. And yet something is literally asserted about a chair when it is said that a chair has arms. Let us imagine a situation in which someone who had never seen a chair before was told what a chair was and that it had arms. Can we suppose that when confronted with a chair he would confuse the arms of the chair with its legs? Probably not, at least, if he knew what human arms were. There is some recognizable similarity between human arms and the arms of certain chairs. But of course the difference is tremendous. The arms of the chair are to the chair as the arms of a man are to a man. And insofar as men differ from chairs, chair arms differ from human arms. It might make sense to ask whether the average arms of a chair are longer than the average arms of a man, but it would be rather odd to ask: which requires more blood transfusions at the loss of an arm, a chair or a man? At times non-literal statements about God appear to end in absurdity, rather than literal statements. For example, Samuel's statement that "God will not lie nor repent: For he is not a man, that he should repent," is certainly meant literally and when so understood

[31] For a more extensive discussion of the problems that are involved here, the reader might consult E.L. Mascall, *Existence and Analogy*, Longmans, Green and Co., London, New York, Toronto, 1949.

precludes views of God that would otherwise lead to absurdity.

When it is said, however, that God is a personal being and man is a personal being, the concept of a personal being need not be ascribed to man and to God in a univocal sense. What is affirmed with respect to God is both literal and analogical. To speak of God as a personal being is not to ascribe to him every trait and characteristic that is ascribed to a man, nor is it entirely different. The sense in which God is a personal being is not wholly other than the sense in which man is a personal being. "Personal being" is not ascribed to God in a purely equivocal manner.

Something is literally asserted about God when it is said that he is personal. Among other things, what is meant is that God is not an unconscious force, but he is a conscious, intelligent being capable of purposive action.

To say that God is a personal being is not to ascribe human weaknesses and defects to God. The personal character of a man is to the nature of man as the personal character of God is to the nature of God. Whatever is ascribed to man and to God differ as the nature of man differs from the nature of God. The limitations and imperfections are to be found on the side of man, while there is no limitation or imperfection that is to be ascribed to God.

No attempt has been made to demonstrate by the discussion of what is meant by saying that "God is a personal being" that there is in fact such a being. It should be apparent, however, that to conceive of God as a personal being does not necessarily imply a lack of sophistication.

Moreover, a second point which is of far greater importance than being sophisticated, whatever that may mean, is that to grant that God is a personal being is to grant the possibility, if not the actuality of revelation.

Among the suppressed premises of anyone that denies the possibility of revelation there is to be found the denial that God is a personal being. To grant that God is personal is to grant the possibility of revelation. To deny that God is personal is to deny the possibility of revelation. The admission of a personal God is equivalent to the admission of the possibility of revelation. The rejection of a personal God is equivalent to the rejection of revelation. There can be revelation, if and only if, there is a personal God.

It is absurd to hold to the possibility of revelation, if, and only if, the prior denial of the existence of a personal God has been made. Otherwise, the question of the actuality of divine revelation remains an open question.

We have now reached the point in our discussion where it is clear that anyone who holds to the existence of a personal God must allow for the possibility of revelation. The problem remains, however, as to how one moves from the notion that there is a God, to the notion that God is personal, and from there to the notion that God has revealed himself.

Anyone who accepts the validity of the arguments put forth in chapter one by Gilson and Maritain, that the existence of God is demonstrable, may be psychologically more willing to identify the God of reason with a revealed, personal God, and yet he, too, must admit that although he is committed to the existential identity of the God of reason and the God of revelation, the way that he knows the one differs from the other as faith differs from rational demonstration.

The person who accepts the statement "God has revealed himself" as being true, will when challenged, usually refer to what he calls his faith.

Why do people believe that God has revealed himself? The words "faith" and "belief" are used in different senses. When used in its weakest sense, the word "faith" refers to such beliefs that are little more than guesses, opinions, or weak convictions which are readily abandoned. Such transitory beliefs lack psychological certainty and conviction. Such weak beliefs and opinions seldom characterizes what is meant by faith in religious matters.

A second usage of the word faith is to be found in connection with beliefs of some importance, and marked by varying degrees of psychological certitude. Such beliefs are usually retained for sometime by the believer and may also concern religious matters. This second type of faith (F_2) shares with the faith (F_1), described in the preceding paragraph, the characteristic that F_1 and F_2 refer to beliefs for which evidence is wholly lacking, or if such evidence exists, the believer is unaware of it. They differ in that the beliefs included in F_1 are transitory, trivial, and unaccompanied by any high degree of conviction, whereas the beliefs referred to by F_2 may be more or less permanent, important, and marked by great psychological conviction.

The term "faith" is used in a third sense, F_3, when it refers to beliefs concerning matters of importance, for which there is evidence sufficient to produce a degree of certainty that scarcely admits any doubt or wavering. F_3 differs from F_1 and F_2 in that the believer who has faith in this third sense bases his convictions upon evidence of which he is aware and which he deems adequate. Faith in this last sense is usually restricted to matters of great importance, and it is frequently such faith that is to be found among religious believers.

A fourth sense of the word faith, a sense employed by Dooyeweerd and Augustine, F_4, does not refer to any particular set of beliefs, but it refers to the phenomenon that human experience is never free from acts of belief in the sense of F_1, F_2, and F_3. There is no area of human experience which is free of beliefs and convictions.

Faith$_4$ refers to the fact that unless faith F_1, F_2, and F_3 are held, knowledge would be impossible. *It is necessary to believe in order to know.* F_4 refers to that aspect of human experience which makes F_1, F_2, and F_3 necessary for all experience.

The universality and necessity of the faith referred to by the term ("F_4") may become evident to the reader if he notes that unless he "believes" in such things as the identity of his own person, the general reliability of his memory, and in the general trustworthiness of his sense experience, he will be unable to read this page. It is well to remember, as anyone familiar with the history of philosophy will recall, that each of the preceding beliefs have been denied at one time or the other.

Consider, for example, the laws of logic. How does one demonstrate the law of non-contradiction: It is false that P (any proposition) is true and that P is not true.[32] To deny this principle leads to absurdity and renders all rational distinctions impossible, but how does one convince someone else that absurdities are impossible? All rational demonstration presupposes the law in question.[33]

The basic principles of logic[34] are rationally intuited. For most people they are accompanied by the highest degree of certainty, and yet the conviction that they are both laws of thought, and that they also hold for the world in which we live rests upon a belief that is analogous to religious faith and which is incapable of demonstration, without presupposing what is in question.

Faith in this fourth sense is to be found in every area of human experience. It varies, however, as one aspect of our experience differs from the other. Faith as it discloses itself in the various shades of conviction within the sciences is, for example, not identical with faith as it appears within the area of religious convictions.

The nature of scientific method and the problem of confirming or disconfirming a scientific hypothesis may help the reader to understand the complexity of the problem. For the demand is often made of the religious believer to produce evidence,

---

[32] By using '∼' to stand for negation, and '•' to stand for the conjunction, this law is frequently written as ∼ (P.∼P).

[33] The reader familiar with logic will recall that the admission of contradictory premises permits the valid demonstration of all absurdities. For example, from the contradictory premises Today is Tuesday and Today is not Tuesday, it can be inferred that either today is Tuesday or The moon is made of sugar, and since Today is not Tuesday, by means of a disjunctive syllogism it validly follows that the moon is made of sugar, and this is indeed very odd, since we could have shown with equal validity that either today is Tuesday or the moon is not made of sugar, and since today is not Tuesday, the moon is not made of sugar.

[34] Examples of the basic principles of logic, are the three laws of thought, the law of non-contradiction, the law of excluded middle, P or not P, and not both, and the law of identity, if P then P.

in support of his beliefs, of such a conclusive nature that if a similar demand were to be made in other fields, the whole body of human knowledge would be dismissed at once as primitive superstition.

The reader familiar with the so-called problem of induction will recall that unless one is willing to admit that it is legitimate to jump from limited experiences of the particular, to the universal, further deductions cannot be validly made. For from two particular premises, no universal statment follows with deductive certainty.[35] It is psychologically possible to remain content with probability, and some take this alternative. Others *"believe"* that the human mind is so constituted that from a limited experience of the particular, the essence of the particular may be grasped in a concept, so that a universal proposition may then be formulated.[36]

The lack of theoretical certitude that is frequently found in connection with the confirmation or disconfirmation of a scientific hypothesis arises for many from the fact that when the formulation of an hypothesis H, permits the prediction a, b, and c to be made, the subsequent realization of a, b, and c does not confirm the initial hypothesis with deductive certainty.[37]

At first it might appear that although it may be impossible to confirm an hypothesis with deductive certainty, it is nevertheless possible to disconfirm an hypothesis with deductive certainty, since if a hypothesis H permits the prediction, a, b, c, and this prediction is not fulfilled, the inference that the hypothesis is false would then validly follow. The situation is,

[35] If the two particular propositions are used as premises in a categorical syllogism, the latter will be invalid in every possible figure and mood. It will either contain an undistributed middle term, or commit the fallacy of illicit process of the major term.

[36] Cf. Henry Veatch, *Intentional Logic,* Yale University Press.

[37] From a purely formal point of view, to infer, If H then a, b, and c, and since a, b, and c, therefore H, is to commit the fallacy of affirming the consequent. It is similar to the argument, If Willie drives his car then Willie is going somewhere, and since we know that Willie is now going somewhere, he must be driving his car. The fallacy is immediately detected if the reader notes that Willie might have decided to walk somewhere.

however, never so simple. For a single simple hypothesis is never formulated. The formulation of an hypothesis is accompanied by a host of tacit assumptions, so if the prediction formulated on the basis of an hypothesis fails to be realized, the conclusion that can be inferred validly is either the initial hypothesis is wrong or the tacit assumptions are wrong, or possibly both are wrong.[38]

The scientific method thus depends in part on certain tacit assumptions. The use of such assumptions and hypotheses are analogous to faith in a religious sense. For although the scientist may be content with theoretical doubt and with probability, he is often from a practical point of view psychologically certain of his results.

We are not suggesting that the situation in science and religion is identical. Nor are we suggesting that because the scientist takes certain things for granted that the theologian has the right to do likewise. The sole point that we would make here is that to demand theoretical certainty in the area of religion is to require more than is required in any other area.

Within the area of religion the very subject matter requires the exercise of faith, and there is a sense in which no one can avoid a certain religious *a priori*. There is a sense in which all men make implicit, if not explicit assumptions about themselves and whatever they hold to be the origin of themselves and of their world, with its many structures and laws. It is the merit of Dooyeweerd's position that he has once again drawn attention to the aspect of faith in our experience.

The object of religion need not be an objective supernatural being; it can be a part of nature, or it can be man himself that is taken to be the origin of all purpose and meaning within our world and our experience. But whatever it is, in the last an-

[38] This can be briefly written:

If (H and T) then (*a* and *b* and *c*)

not (*a* and *b* and *c*)

Therefore, not (H and T)

That is, not H or not T

Where H is the initial hypothesis, T=tacit assumptions, and *a*, *b*, *c*, predicted results.

alysis, the choice that is made at least in part is due to the faith which one has.[39]

Such a faith is usually not solely an individual matter; it is shared by many others. At a given time within a certain community, certain common beliefs are held by its members with such conviction that they are never questioned. The acceptance of such commonly held beliefs are often the necessary prerequisite for belonging to the community.

It is well to note in conclusion that those who deny the possibility of theology often take the presence of "evil" as evidence for their position. The Christian is frequently challenged by statements and questions such as:

"The presence of evil in the universe is incompatible with the existence of God."

"The existence of a wise, omnipotent, loving heavenly power is incompatible with the evil condition of the world."

"How can a good God permit the anguished cry of a single innocent child?"

"How can there be evil men like Eichman, Hitler and Stalin, if God is in the heavens?"

Such sentences, however, either make no sense or they presuppose the points at issue in such a manner that they in no wise constitute evidence against Biblical religion.

There are, of course, those who would deny that there is an objective basis for religion and also deny that there is evil in the world. There can be no problem of reconciling God and evil if the reality of both are denied. There can also be no problem of reconciliation if evil is thought to be real and the reality of God is denied, nor if the reality of evil is denied and

---

[39] For an extensive argument in support of this essentially Augustinian thesis the reader is again referred to H. Dooyeweerd, *A New Critique of Theoretical Thought*, Vol. I, Presbyterian and Reformed Publishing Co. 1957

God alone is thought to be real. The problem of theodicy, of reconciling the reality of God and the reality of evil occurs if and only if there is a dualism between two ultimate metaphysical principles, namely God and evil.

Consider the first of the preceding statements: "The presence of evil in the universe is incompatible with the existence of God." What is here meant by the term "evil"? Does the reader understand this sentence?

To understand what the term "evil" means, we first need to discover how people do in fact use it. It is easy to assume that the above statement is readily understood and that everyone understands the same thing by it. The term "evil" is frequently used to refer to what is detrimental to or destructive of living organisms. Evil may be identified with whatever causes or contributes to suffering or it may simply be equated with physical suffering and/or death.

The term "evil" is used in a second sense when it is said that a particular person is evil or that a certain act is evil. Here the term is used in a *moral sense* to describe an act which *ought* not to have been performed or to describe what is judged to be an undesirable character.

Now in addition to the physical and moral senses in which the word evil is used, the term is thought to have a "metaphysical" sense. The question is asked, What is evil? And, then when such answers are given that cancer is evil, because it destroys human life; that Hitler was evil because he murdered innocent people; the questioner snaps back, "but that is not what I want to know. I want to know what *evil* is"? And then both the questioner and the answerer do not know what to say. They are both puzzled, profoundly puzzled, but puzzled. Maybe "evil is a privation," says the one. No says the other, "It's equally ultimate with the good." "Ah," says the third, looking very wise, "How is the presence of evil compatible with an all powerful God"? And so on and on it goes. We chase the word "evil," looking for a thing behind a word, a game of hide-and-seek-a-thing-behind-a-word, a metaphysical scrabble, a cosmic grab bag. Step up and pull out a substance in return for a substantive! Hurry it may be your last chance.

Consider a parallel situation in which the question is asked: What is strength? The answer is given that John has strength, because he can lift more horseshoes than any other blacksmith. Other similar answers are given in which even greater feats are mentioned. The questioner understands every answer. He, too, know "What strength *is*"? Now just what is it that he wants to knows how to use the word "strength," but he still wants to know? What is it that he does not already know. Why is he puzzled? What question would he know the answer to if someone *could* tell him "What strength *really* is"? What sort of answer would satisfy him? He has already rejected the only proper answer. Why then does he keep asking? Perhaps he's curious. The oysters were curious. It's very odd to be curious unless you are curious *about* something.

What is one curious about when he asks: What is evil? The question makes no sense, unless the questioner is satisfied with such answers as: Death is evil, pain is evil, Hitler is evil. Of course, the word evil may be given new usages, but evil is not a thing or event over and above the things and events that we experience. The word may be given a meaning when it is used to refer to certain acts, events, and to certain people, but it has no meaning when the word "evil" is used to refer to evil. For evil is not a thing distinct from certain concrete states of affairs.

Upon closer examination the sentence, "The presence of evil in the universe is incompatible with the existence of God," makes no sense if "evil" is used in its so-called metaphysical sense. For the term "evil" here simply fails to designate. It is as if one were to say: "The presence of boojums is incompatible with the existence of God," without first explaining what is meant by a boojum.

If the word "evil" is used in its physical or moral sense, the sentences under consideration are at least intelligible. It then remains to be seen whether physical suffering, death and men like Hitler are incompatible with the God of Biblical revelation.

Do pain and evil men constitute evidence against the God of the Bible?

In what sense is physical and moral evil incompatible with the God of Biblical religion? Is there anything about physical and moral evil that necessitates the non-existence of the Biblical God? If so, what is it? Rather, one should ask, what is there about the nature of the Biblical God which would require a universe without physical and moral evil?

It is to be noted first of all that unless the Biblical God is accepted, moral evil is reducible to likes and dislikes. For unless God is the author of moral norms, what is meant by saying that "Hitler is evil."

There are three possible sources of moral standards, God, man, and physical nature. If God is eliminated man and nature alone remain. Moral standards or norms can then be derived either from man or nature. It is difficult to see how nature can help. Neither rocks, rivers, rattlesnakes, planets, plants, nor even little fish can tell man what he ought to do. What is "nature"? The word is sometimes hypostatized and used as though it referred to something other than sticks and stones, "Mother Nature"! We have already seen that persons alone are capable of free conscious, purposive behavior.

Unless nature is personified, when God is rejected, man alone is the standard of what is right and wrong. Since men differ in what they want, there are then as many possible standards as there are human differences. The terms "right" and "wrong" may then be used to refer to the feelings that a particular person has with respect to a particular action, what pleases the individual or groups of individuals, or they may simply be terms in a shared language. "If there is no God, then in a moral sense, all things are possible." Of course, the values that are then adopted may be the same values that were in vogue when men thought God existed. In business, honesty may still be the best policy; stealing, lying, murder, rape, and pillage, do not help everyone, and without God one can still live as though God has said, "Thou shalt not." When a particular individual or group of individuals persists in acting contrary to the norms accepted by the majority, or by those in power, sanctions may be imposed against the non-conformists. To say that Eichman or Hitler were wrong means that according to the usually accepted standards of Western Society, Eichman and Hitler were wrong. They violated the commonly held moral norms. In other words, "we don't like Hitler and Eichman;" "why"? Because they killed people without any reason, "and we don't like killing because after people are killed, they are dead," "But, what is wrong with dead people"? "We like them alive better." The problem, of course, was that Eichman didn't, a slight difference of opinion between Eichman and six million Jews.

The point is that unless moral standards have the approval and sanction of God, unless God is the moral law-giver, there are no unchanging moral standards. Moral evil is simply what certain people do not like. Most people do not like suffering and death, so in most cases, moral evil will be identified with physical evil.

If moral evil is reducible to what "Adam and his brothers" don't like, it is difficult to see how "The presence of evil in the universe is incompatible with the existence of God." For if "evil" is used in its moral sense, it then means that what "Adam and his brothers don't like is incompatible with the existence of God." The likes and dislikes of Adam and his kinfolk do not necessitate the existence or non-existence of anything.

If God is denied, what remains is personal likes and dislikes and physical evil, that is suffering and death. What does it mean, however, to call suffering and death evil? Here, too, if God is denied, evil is what most men other than sadists do not like. What else can "evil" here mean other than what people don't like? And what is there about human likes and dislikes that is incompatible with the Biblical God?

Perhaps what is really meant in saying that the evil condition of the world is incompatible with an omniscient, omnipotent God is simply the "modest" admission that "if I were God I would do things differently." The world is a place in which physical death and suffering occur. It is not a place where there are, however, anguished innocent cries, not if Biblical revelation is true.

The Bible does have an answer for the presence of physical suffering and death. Death and pain are God's punishment for man's disobedience. The non-believer may neither like or believe the Biblical answer, but, then what answer does the non-believer have? To die is as normal as to live.

The Bible does have an explanation of "evil". It denies metaphysical evil; it regards physical pain and death as the result of man's own act of disobedience.

Men like Hitler, and death and pain do not constitute evidence against the God of Biblical revelation; the latter provides rather a basis for the condemnation of Hitler and it offers an escape from the consequences of sin, namely, eternal life.[40]

Thus it is clear that those who deny the possibility of theology, because they hold that there is no God capable of revealing himself, and those that affirm their faith in revelation, *both constitute a community of believers.* In the last analysis, at least part of their reasons for looking at theology the way they do depends upon their basic faith and commitments. Such faith may be held to on the basis of evidence or in the absence of evidence. How then are philosophy and theology related? The way in which this question is answered will depend primarily upon how we answer the question: What is theology? And what we consider theology to be will depend upon whether we accept a revelation from God, and whether we accept a given revelation from God depends in the last analysis upon whether we believe that God has in fact revealed himself.

The issue which is of primary concern is not whether philosophy and theology are regarded as completely distinct, but whether they are able to arrive at true propositions, propositions about God, man, and the world.

---

[40] For a fuller treatment of Revelation and Morality see Gordon H. Clark, *Religion, Reason and Revelation,* Presbyterian and Reformed Publishing Co. 1961, especially pp. 151 to 191.

Dooyeweerd has repeatedly pointed out, "a complex of subjective prejudices" are asserted as *"theoretical axioms,"* i.e., "the prejudice about the autonomy of theoretical thought, that about the spontaneity of understanding (the logical function of thought) as a formal legislator in respect to 'nature,' that about understanding and sense as the two sole sources of knowledge, and that about the identity of 'object' and theoretic *Gegenstand,* etc." The presuppositions of these "theoretical axioms" are always religious presuppositions which represent acts of faith.

All these dogmatic prejudices are in their mutual connection ruled by a *basic-prejudice,* that turns out to have no philosophical character at all, and that should be unmasked by a real transcendental criticism of philosophical thought.[41]

Philosophical *theoria* which began its history as a new autonomous religion in ancient Greece must be recognized to have still in its unacknowledged heart, presuppositions which are religious. Can philosophies which fail to recognize their own acts of faith hope to cope with the question of the relationship of philosophy and theology?

[41] H. Dooyeweerd: *Transcendental Problems of Philosophic Thought,* P. 20 f. Grand Rapids: Eerdmans, 1948.